Activities Manual
to accompany

The Education of Character
Lessons for Beginners

Will Keim

Prepared by

Tim McMahon
Western Illinois University

Barbara Panzl
Whitman College

Peter Simonds
College of the Holy Cross

Harcourt Brace College Publishers
Fort Worth Philadelphia New York Orlando Austin San Antonio
Toronto Montreal London Sydney Toyko

ISBN: 0-15-502190-7

Copyright © 1995 by Harcourt Brace & Company

All rights reserved. No part of this publication may be reproduced or transmitted in any form or by any means, electronic or mechanical, including photocopy, recording, or any information storage and retrieval system, without permission in writing from the publisher.

Requests for permission to make copies of any part of the work should be mailed to: Permissions Department, Harcourt Brace & Company, 6277 Sea Harbor Drive, Orlando, Florida 32887-6777.

Address editorial correspondence to:
Harcourt Brace College Publishers
301 Commerce Street, Suite 3700
Fort Worth, TX 76102

Address orders to:
Harcourt Brace & Company
6277 Sea Harbor Drive
Orlando, Fl 32887-6777
1-800-782-4479
1-800-433-0001 (in Florida)

Printed in the United States of America
5 6 7 8 9 0 1 2 3 4 129 0 9 8 7 6 5 4 3 2 1

FOREWORD

Congratulations! You have just begun what is sure to be one of the most amazing times in your life—your college education. Your years in college will be like no other period in your life. At no other time will you be surrounded by so many people dedicated to helping you learn and develop as a human being. But even with all this support, sometimes the challenges will seem overwhelming. Some days will be filled with moments you will treasure your entire life. Other days will seem equally awful. This is the nature of college life. It is like an emotional roller coaster, with huge ups and downs. Through it all, this book will be of great help on your journey.

As personal friends of Will Keim, Barbara, Peter and Tim are excited about your reading and using this workbook to help you along the way. We believe that these exercises will enable you to gain the most from your college experience and get you started on your way to fulfilling your dreams. If you involve yourself in these experiences, the time will be wisely spent and the results will be undeniable.

Again, our hearty best wishes for a successful, happy, healthy, and safe college experience. It is truly an amazing time in your life!

Barabara Panzl
Peter Simonds
Tim McMahon

Table of Contents

Foreword		iii
General Activities		1
Lesson 1	Life	10
Lesson 2	Culture	19
Lesson 3	Pain	27
Lesson 4	Passion	35
Lesson 5	Purpose	42
Lesson 6	Yourself	48
Lesson 7	Education	54
Lesson 8	Finances	59
Lesson 9	Consumerism	65
Lesson 10	Parents	73
Lesson 11	Freshman	78
Lesson 12	Experience	85
Lesson 13	Attendance	92
Lesson 14	Studying	99
Lesson 15	Major	105
Lesson 16	Stress	112
Lesson 17	Alcohol	119
Lesson 18	Drugs	127
Lesson 19	Sex	134
Lesson 20	Dating	141
Lesson 21	Wellness	150
Lesson 22	Ethics	157
Lesson 23	Hate	164
Lesson 24	Spirituality	174
Lesson 25	Seniors	180
Lesson 26	Homecoming	187

Lesson 27	Contributorship	193
Lesson 28	Success	200
Lesson 29	Warriorship	205
Lesson 30	Love	212
Lesson 31	Fear	221
Lesson 32	Loneliness	228
Lesson 33	Happiness	234

General Activities

The Me I Want To Be
Four Years From Now

Purpose   To identify the academic and co-curricular goals you would like to accomplish while a student in college.

Objective   To dream about what you most want to accomplish during your college career, and to begin to set goals that will start you on the path to making these dreams a reality before you graduate.

Instructions   1.   Picture yourself as a graduating senior 4 - 5 years from now. What would you like to have accomplished academically? In which organizations and activities would you like to have been involved? What do you need to do to prepare yourself for a career? What do you want to experience personally and socially?

2.   Reflecting on that image of yourself 4 - 5 years from now, what goals and objectives can you set for yourself to accomplish in the next few months, that will get you started toward what you hope to have accomplished 4 - 5 years in the future? List these starting goals and objectives below:

Concluding Remarks

Although 4 - 5 years might seem like plenty of time to accomplish everything you want to do while at college, the time will go by rapidly. It is easy to lose sight of your goals when dealing with tests and papers. By taking time to envision who you want to be 4 - 5 years from now, you can begin making deliberate choices today that start you moving in the direction you want to head. After you complete this activity, ask yourself the following questions:

a. Was it difficult or easy to picture yourself 4 - 5 years from now as a graduating senior? Why?
b. Was it difficult or easy to identify what you would like to have accomplished academically and co-curricularly 4 - 5 years from now? Why?
c. What struck you most about yourself 4 - 5 years from now?
d. Are you likely to follow-through on the goals you listed above? Why or why not?

STUDENT SERVICES
WALKING CAMPUS TOUR

Purpose To identify the on-campus services and resources available to you as a student on campus.

Objective To use your campus map and campus telephone book to identify, locate, and visit a variety of services resources on your college campus.

Supplies Campus map and campus telephone book.

Instructions
1. Look through the campus telephone book at all the services available at your institution and highlight the various on-campus services you might want to take advantage of during the next several years. Make sure you think about all the possible situations that could happen to you: loss of a job, an illness or accident on campus, looking toward your future after college, problems with a faculty member, etc. Make a list of those services that will help you (i.e. health center, career center, library, gym, etc.).

2. Use a campus map to identify the location of these different facilities.

3. To familiarize yourself with the exact location of each service, take a walking tour of campus and locate the office/building of each service.

4. When you complete your walking tour, use the campus directory to identify the name of the director of each service and an office telephone number. Finally, if you have questions for any of the services you located, either stop by the office or call in advance and schedule an appointment with the director.

Concluding Remarks During your 4 - 5 years on campus, there will be many services and resources of which you will want to take advantage. By identifying these services and resources now, at the start of your college career, you will never miss an opportunity to utilize these programs in the future due to a lack of knowledge. Before you can take advantage of these services, however, you have to be aware that these services exist. By identifying the types of services you may want to take advantage of at any point in your college career, you will at least be aware that these services exist, even if you do not take advantage of them during your first year on campus. By knowing what is available, you also support your ability to take advantage of the many diverse opportunities that these services provide for you to get involved on campus and develop leadership skills and other interests. After you complete this activity, ask yourself the following questions:

a.   Were you surprised by how many services were available to you? Which service did you identify that you were most surprised to find on campus?
b.   How do you feel about using these services? Would you be comfortable walking in and asking questions of the staff? Why or why not?
c.   What advantages can you see in knowing where a service such as the career center is now, even if you do not plan to graduate for several years?

MY GREATEST HOPES
MY GREATEST FEARS

Purpose   To identify and share your greatest hopes and fears for yourself while at college.

Objective   To connect and share with another person your greatest hopes and fears and find an ally in meeting your hopes and overcoming your fears.

Instructions   1.   Answer the following questions: a) What are your greatest hopes for yourself while at college? b) What are your greatest fears for yourself while at college?

2.   Ask your roommate or a close friend these same two questions and share your responses with each other.

3. At the start of your second semester, sit down with your roommate or close friend and again ask each other these two questions. If your responses have changed, share with each other why your hopes and fears may have changed after a semester in college.

Concluding Remarks

Everyone comes to college with hopes and fears. Unfortunately, we often think that we are the only person on campus who packed these two things and brought them to college with us. By sharing these things with someone else, you realize that you are not alone in feeling both a bit scared and hopeful. Hopefully, you now have someone who can provide you with encouragement and support as you try to overcome your fears and make your hopes a reality through your experiences in college. After you complete this activity, ask yourself the following questions:

a. Were you aware of your own personal hopes and fears before this activity?
b. Was it difficult to ask your roommate or a close friend to share in this activity with you? How did sharing this information with that person make you feel?
c. Do you think your hopes and fears will change by the beginning of next semester? next year? Why or why not?
d. Did you learn anything about yourself from reflecting on your personal hopes and fears?
e. What do you want to do with this information on your hopes and fears now that you have it?

RECREATIONAL ACTIVITIES IDENTIFICATION

Purpose To identify several recreational activities that are of interest to you and in which you enjoy participating.

Objective To develop a list of activities that you enjoy doing and to find out where to do them.

Instructions 1. List several recreational activities in which you enjoy participating (i.e. biking, going to the movies, basketball, etc.) and identify which of these activities are available a) on the campus and b) in the local community.

2. Create an action plan for exploring each recreational activity of interest to you by finding out the following information:

Location:

Cost:

Distance from campus:

Directions (if necessary):

Others who might enjoy the same activity:

Concluding Remarks

By investing a small amount of time to investigate your recreational options now, you will never be at a loss for something to do when you actually have free time. You can avoid feeling bored because you will have the information at your fingertips about how and where to satisfy your recreational needs. By identifying others who enjoy the same interests you do, you will also have a variety of people to share in the activities with you. After you complete this activity, ask yourself the following questions:

a. Are recreational activities important to you? What need might these activities play in your college career?
b. Were you aware of how many recreational options were available to you on campus? Are you likely to take advantage of these activities? Why or why not?
c. Have you found any new activities that are available that you would like to try? What would encourage you to test out a new recreational activity?

LESSON 1

LIFE

CHANGE ONE THING

Purpose To change some aspect of your life.

Objectives To identify one aspect of your life that you would really like to change and to develop a plan to change this aspect.

Time Ongoing throughout the term.

Instructions Think about one of your behaviors that you would like to change the most. Then complete the worksheet below:

What behavior would you like to change? (Try to be as specific as possible.)

By what date would you like this change to occur? (Try to be as specific as possible.)

How would your life be different if this behavior was changed?

Lesson 1 Life

What obstacles might prevent you from making this change?

What are three things you can do on a **daily** basis to help make this behavior change really occur?

1.

2.

3.

How will you celebrate changing this behavior?

Lesson 1 Life

Now write out a one sentence statement that you can easily remember and will "affirm" your desire to make this change. (for example—I'm working hard to get into shape.)

3. Review your worksheet. Make any additions or deletions that seem appropriate.

4. Use your worksheet as a blueprint for making this change. Remember that long term change happens by changing daily behaviors.

Concluding Remarks

Remember that change is difficult—the old ways you did things will not be easily discarded. Hang in there; it usually takes over three weeks to establish a new habit so you've got to be in it for the long term. Good luck in your change process. After you have completed this activity, ask yourself the following questions:

a. What other behaviors can you change by doing this activity?
b. Why are some behaviors easier to change than others?

Lesson 1 Life

YOUR CIRCLE OF INFLUENCE

Purpose To help differentiate those aspects of your life over which you have control and those of which you can only influence.

Objectives To identify those parts of your life over which you have control and those parts over which you do not have control, then to determine the implications of letting go of the parts over which you have no control.

Instructions
1. Inside the inner, smaller circle in the diagram below write down aspects of your life which you can control. This could include what you eat, how you spend your time, your major, etc.
2. Inside the outer, larger circle in the diagram below put some aspects of your life which you cannot control. This could include your gender, your parents, your race or ethnicity, etc.

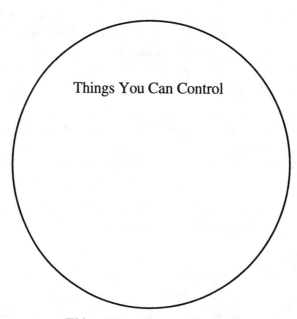

Things You Cannot Control

Lesson 1 Life

3. Now pair up with someone sitting close to you and discuss what you've placed inside your circles. Add things to your circles that you may have forgotten to include.

4. As a class, discuss the following questions:

Over what parts of your life do you really have complete control?

Over what parts of your life do you have partial control?

What happens when you try to control other people? When other people try to control you?

Lesson 1 Life

Concluding Remarks

The world around us often seems chaotic and out of control. This is the way the universe functions. In the modern world, it is not possible to be "anal retentive" and function effectively. No matter how hard you try, you cannot control those things which will drive you nuts. We all focus precious time and energy on aspects of our lives over which we really have no control. After you complete this activity, ask yourself the following questions:

a. How much control do I like to have over situations?
b. How can I maintain the level of control I want over the things inside the smaller circle?
c. Why do you think some people need more control over their lives while other people are more laid back?

JOURNAL ENTRY ON LIFE

College is a time of ups and downs. Some days, you'll feel on top of the world. On others, life will seem very, very difficult or sad. It can help to remember to focus on the positive things that you enjoy in life. Take this opportunity to write down your thoughts related to the following statement—"The Things I Enjoy Most In Life." Keep this journal entry for those times in which the world seems a bit harder to face.

RESOURCES

Bach, R. (1984). <u>The Bridge Across Forever</u>. New York: Dell.

Brooks, S. (1990). <u>The Art of Good Living</u>. Boston: Houghton Mifflin.

Covey, S. (1989). <u>The 7 Habits of Highly Effective People</u>. New York: Simon and Schuster.

Cxikszentmiahalyi, M. (1990. <u>Flow</u>. New York: Harper & Row.

de Saint Exupery, A. (1943). <u>The Little Prince</u>. New York: Harcourt, Brace & World.

Gibran, K. (1975). <u>The Prophet</u>. New York: Alfred A. Knopf.

John-Roger & McWilliams, P. (1990). <u>Do It!</u> Los Angeles: Prelude.

Keen, S. and Valley-Fox, A. (1989). <u>Your Mythic Journey</u>. Los Angeles: Jeremy P. Tarcher.

Maclean, N. (1976). <u>A River Runs Through It</u>. Chicago: University of Chicago.

Myers, D. (1992). <u>The Pursuit of Happiness</u>. New York: Avon.

Peck, M. (1987). <u>The Different Drum</u>. New York: Simon and Schuster.

Peck, M. (1992). <u>A World Waiting to Be Born</u>. New York: Bantam.

Lesson 2

CULTURE

CHALLENGING YOUR STEREOTYPES

Purpose To become aware of your commonly held stereotypes and recognize how fear and lack of understanding perpetuate beliefs that have little or no basis in truth and can be harmful.

Objective To list stereotypes of a group of which you are a member and then identify ways you do not fit those stereotypes. Then to list stereotypes that you hold of a group and identify ways that members of that group do not fit those stereotypes.

Instructions 1. Identify a group you belong to for which stereotypes exist. Examples could include groups such as athletes, Greeks, women, Asian Americans, small town residents, etc. List as many stereotypes as you can think of that relate to your group.

Group:

Stereotypes:

2. Review each stereotype that you have listed and where appropriate, write an example of how the stereotype does not fit you.

Lesson 2   Culture

3. Select any one group about which you have stereotypes and list as many of the stereotypes as you can.

Group:

Stereotypes:

4. Identify a person from your "stereotyped" group and explain to this person that you are attempting to increase your awareness and understanding by challenging commonly held stereotypes. Ask if he or she would be willing to talk with you about these stereotypes. As you review each stereotype, jot down notes or examples that disprove or contradict the stereotype.

Concluding Remarks

This exercise requires you to actively reach out and challenge your perceptions of a group for which there exists a stereotypical perception. While this is a risk, you will gain a much more accurate view of the person from the group with whom you talk and realize that few members of that group actually have the characteristics, attitudes, or behaviors that the stereotypes attribute to all group members. After you complete this activity, ask yourself the following questions:

a. How did this exercise make you feel?
b. How do you think the person you talked with felt about being asked about the stereotypes?
c. What did you learn from this activity?
d. What realization did you have when you found you could disprove the stereotypes about the group in which you identified yourself?
e. How does what you learned from the person with whom you talked relate to the stereotypes you might have about other groups?
f. How will you react/what will you do when you hear other people make comments about the stereotypes you have disproven?

CULTURAL DIVERSITY AFFIRMATIONS

Purpose To acknowledge the things you enjoy that have been given to you by different cultures and affirm the people who share them with you.

Objective To list some of the things you enjoy most from other cultures or countries and acknowledge how these things add fun or joy to your life.

Instructions
1. Under each of the categories listed in the chart on the following page, there are two sentence stems you are being asked to complete. The first sentence stem states, "I enjoy..." and in this space you have the opportunity to list any activities, foods, holidays, events, etc. that the people in this category have contributed to our culture.

2. The second sentence stem states, "I appreciate these things because..." and under this space you have the opportunity to voice how and why you appreciate their contributions to our cultural diversity.

Concluding Remarks Every population group that lives in the United States has added to our country through contributions of food, music, accomplishments and celebrations. This diversity of experiences has made each of our lives richer by providing us with a rainbow of choices. By taking a few minutes to acknowledge the contributions different groups have made to our over-all cultural diversity, you affirm these groups and provide yourself with an ever greater enjoyment of their contributions. After you complete this activity, ask yourself the following questions:

a. Was it easier to think of things you enjoyed from some groups than for others? Why do you think this might be true?
b. Was it difficult to articulate why you appreciated these things?
c. Will completing this activity make your enjoyment of these activities different? Why or why not?

	African-Americans
I enjoy...	
I appreciate these things because...	

	Asian-Americans
I enjoy...	
I appreciate these things because...	

	Euro-Americans
I enjoy...	
I appreciate these things because...	

	Hispanic/Mexican-Americans
I enjoy...	
I appreciate these things because...	

	Native-Americans
I enjoy...	
I appreciate these things because...	

JOURNAL ENTRY ON DIVERSITY

Reflect on a personal situation where your presence provided the only diversity in a group. How did your being different from everyone else make you feel? How did you act? How did other group members react to you?

RESOURCES

Astin, A. W. (1982). <u>Minorities in American Higher Education</u>. San Francisco: Jossey-Bass.

Bafa Bafa (A Cross Culture Simulation Game). (1977). Simile II, 218 Twelfth Street, P.O. Box 910, Del Mar, CA 92014.

Banks, J. A. (1988). <u>Multiethnic Education</u>. Newton, MA: Allyn and Bacon, Inc.

Intercultural Press, Inc. P.O. Box 700, Yarmouth, Maine 04096, (207)-846-5168, (207)-846-5181 (FAX). (Features books, simulations and videos on issues of diversity, multiculturalism, interculturalism and international relations.)

Kanter, R. M. <u>A Tale of "O:" On Being Different in an Organization.</u>. NY: Harper and Row. (out of print, available in libraries).

LMA Inc. does consulting and training in managing cultural and gender diversity as part of their mission of "bringing organization into the future." They are located at 365 Melendy Road, Milford, NH, 03055.

Mintz, S. D. (Ed.). (1993). <u>Sources: Diversity Initiatives in Higher Education</u>. Washington, D.C.: American Council on Education.

Simons, G. (1989). <u>Working Together: How to Become More Effective in a Multicultural Organization.</u>. Los Altos, CA: Crisp Publications, Inc.

Trotter, T. & Allen, J. (1993). <u>602 Ways to Build and Promote Racial Harmony</u>. Saratoga, CA: R & E Publishers.

LESSON 3

PAIN

LIFE CAN BE A REAL PAIN

Purpose To share the pain and joy in your life and understand and appreciate the pain and joy in others' lives.

Objective In a group setting, to write down and share your painful moments and joyful moments. With one person you will discuss painful and joyful moments in more depth.

Supplies Index cards, and calming music

Instructions
1. Put on some quiet, soothing music.

2. Take an index card and draw a horizontal line across it dividing it in half lengthwise.

3. On the top half of the card, write down a particularly painful moment or situation in your life which you would be willing to share with another member of the group. It could be divorced parents, problem drinking, eating disorders, drunk driving deaths, financial instability or even an embarrassing moment.

4. On the bottom half of the card, write down a particularly joyous moment in your life. It could be high school graduation, marriage, birth of a child, or even an especially good day.

5. Once all the students in the group have finished their cards, pair up with the person you know least and silently read your partner's card.

6. After three to five minutes, pair up with the next person you know least and read his/her card.

7. Continue this process until you have paired up and read the cards of four or five other students.

8. Now go back to the person whose index card most interested you and have a five to seven minute discussion with him or her concerning their painful and joyous moments. Discuss what made these moments particularly painful or joyous and how each of you handled them.

9. After this conversation, as time permits, repeat this process with two or three other people. Notice the many ways people handle pain and joy.

Concluding Remarks

Pain is a part of living. Without painful moments, the highs wouldn't seem as wonderful. You must learn to accept all that life sends your way and learn from it. To paraphrase the "Master of Possibilities," Robert Schuller, "Say farewell to pain and failure, and hello to joy and success." After you complete this activity, ask yourself the following questions:

a. How did this exercise make you feel about your own personal pain?
b. Did you find your pain put in perspective by hearing the stories of other students' pains?
c. How can you learn to gain solace in your joy and the joy of others?

PAIN IN THE MEDIA

Purpose To experience the feelings surrounding painful moments in the lives of characters in books and movies, and to understand how these characters dealt with their pain.

Objective In a group setting members will have a discussion surrounding painful issues and develop methods for dealing with them.

Instructions 1. The class should break into three groups based on individual interest in each of the following topics, while providing equal numbers for each group.

2. There will be three topics of painful issues. The issues are:

a. Unrequited love
b. Man's inhumanity to his fellow man
c. Homesickness

3. Each one of these groups will use a contemporary cultural form as a starting point for discussing these painful issues. These cultural forms and their salient issues will be as follows:

a. Unrequited love: *The Bridges of Madison County* by Robert James Waller. In this short book, a stranger comes to a small town in the Midwest to take photos of covered bridges. He meets a married woman whose husband and children are away for a few days. They have a love affair. The major painful issue is whether the wife should have left her family responsibilities to purse this great love affair of her life. She did not. The questions surrounding this painful issue are:

Should she have left her family?

Why did she stay with her family?

What would you have done in this same situation?

Why can love be so exhilarating and painful?

b. Man's inhumanity to his fellow man: *Schindler's List* by Thomas Keneally, which has been made into a chilling move by Steven Spielberg. In this book and movie, a German industrialist save the lives of many Jewish people from the Holocaust. The major painful issue is why so few people helped the Jewish people escape the Holocaust and why so many Nazis committed the atrocities of the Holocaust. The questions surrounding this painful issue are:

> Why does it seem so easy to hate people for their race, religion or ethnic background?
>
> Why is the world still get engulfed in holocausts such as those in Bosnia, Northern Ireland, Africa, Middle East, etc.
>
> As Rodney King said, "Why can't people just get along?"
>
> Why is it so hard to love your neighbor as yourself?

c. Homesickness: *The Wizard of Oz*. In this classic movie, Dorothy (Judy Garland) is whisked away by a "tornado" to the Land of Oz from her home in Kansas. Her only hope of returning to her home is by the magic of the Great Oz. While she makes wonderful friends along the way - the Tin Man, the Scarecrow, and the Cowardly Lion - her quest is to be reunited with her family in Kansas. The major painful issue is why Dorothy felt the need for adventure, yet when she got it, she really only wanted to be home. The questions surrounding this painful issue are:

> Why are Dorothy's new-found friends and exciting adventures not enough?
>
> Why are we always searching for "somewhere over the rainbow"?
>
> Why is homesickness so painful?
>
> What can you do to relieve homesickness?

4. Each group should elect a recorder who will take notes and make a presentation on the discussion surrounding these three painful issues to the other groups.

Concluding Remarks

These painful situations are just three of the many that could have been discussed. Life is a series of painful and joyous moments. None of you is suffering more or less pain. Each of you has a unique experience with your own personal pain. The goal is not to eliminate pain, but to develop methods for overcoming it when it arises. After you complete this activity, ask yourself the following questions:

a. Have all people experienced similar pain surrounding certain issues?
b. Does experiencing pain make joyous moments more sweet?
c. How can people learn to accept and conquer pain in their daily lives?

JOURNAL ENTRY ON PAIN

Everyone has some painful moments in their life. Pain is a part of life just like joy. It is what you learn from your painful moments that is important. Some of the lessons you learn are accurate, while others may be faulty. It is important for you to try to tell the difference between accurate and inaccurate conclusions. Think of some of the more painful moments in your life. Why were these moments so painful? What effect did these moments have on your personality? Have the painful moments taught you helpful or harmful lessons? Are these lessons helping or hurting your personal development? How can you overcome inaccurate conclusions?

RESOURCES

Schuller, Robert H. (1988). <u>Success Is Never Ending, Failure Is Never Final</u>. Nashville, TN: Thomas Nelson Publishers.

LESSON 4
PASSION

WHAT ARE YOUR PASSIONS?

Purpose To explore some of the passions that you have in your life.

Objectives To identify pieces of music and writing that inspire you and to communicate those feelings to others

Supplies (Optional: Portable CD player and cassette tape player.)

Instructions

1. Identify a piece of music and a particular writing that are very powerful to you—that give you chills or inspire you. Listen to the music and read the piece of writing.

Music:

Writing:

2. Before you come to class, write a paragraph describing how you feel about the music and another paragraph describing how you feel about the writing. What makes each of these pieces special to you?

3. Bring the writing to class and everyone will have the opportunity to read their favorite pieces and talk about why they are special. (As an optional activity, your instructor may ask you to bring a CD or tape of your piece of music to class and play some of it.)

Concluding Remarks The arts, including music, art, and literature, are a source of passion for many people. In this exercise, you identified portions of the arts that are special to you and heard from

36   Lesson 4   Passion

classmates about what was special for them. After you complete this exercise ask yourself the following questions:

a.   Sometimes it is fun to learn more about the passions of others. What music or writing did you hear in class that you might want to check out for yourself?

b.   How can you keep this music and writing a part of your life?

The Most Important People, Places, Things, and Activities in My Life

Purpose To put your life in perspective by identifying and prioritizing the parts of your life for which you feel most passionate.

Objectives To identify at least five people, places, or activities/things about which you are passionate and to discuss ways to nurture these most important things.

Instructions 1.   Think for a couple minutes about what the most important things in your life are. This could include people, places, things, or activities. Try to generate as long a list as possible—at least five people, five places, and five things or activities.

	People	Places	Things/Activities
1.			
2.			
3.			
4.			
5.			

2.   From these lists, pick the three most important items in each list.
3.   From these three, pick **the** most important person, **the** most important place, and **the** most important thing or activity.
4.   Now consider your most important person, place, and thing or activity. Write a paragraph describing who or what they are and what you do to help them remain active in your life?

Lesson 4   Passion

5. Find pictures of your most important person, place, and thing and bring them to class. Pick one to share in class discussion.

Concluding Remarks

We all have many people, places, and things that are important to us. In an ever-changing world, it is helpful to remember these most important aspects in our lives because they provide us with inspiration, hope, and support. They are, in many ways, the core for our existence. It is also important to remember that they need to be periodically nurtured and fed in order to remain active in our lives. After you complete this activity, ask yourself the following questions:

a. Am I happy with the role these important people, places, things or activities have in my life? Why or why not?

b. How can I make sure that I evaluate periodically what is most important in my life and continue to nurture those things?

JOURNAL ENTRY ON PASSION

Think about an activity or cause about which you are passionate. This could be a sport, political issue, or just something that you really love to do. In your journal, describe this particular activity or cause. Why are you passionate about it? How did you first get interested in this particular activity or cause? How do you hope to continue this interest while in college?

RESOURCES

Bach, R. (1984). The Bridge Across Forever. New York: Dell.

Brooks, S. (1990). The Art of Good Living. Boston: Houghton Mifflin.

Coleman, E. and Edwards, B. (1979). Brief Encounters. Garden City, NY: Anchor.

Covey, S. (1989). The 7 Habits of Highly Effective People. New York: Simon and Schuster.

Cxikszentmiahalyi, M. (1990). Flow. New York: Harper & Row.

John-Roger & McWilliams, P. (1990). Do It! Los Angeles: Prelude.

Maclean, N. (1976). A River Runs Through It. Chicago: University of Chicago.

Myers, D. (1992). The Pursuit of Happiness. New York: Avon.

LESSON 5
PURPOSE

HOW PASSION CAN DEFINE PURPOSE

Purpose To determine how passion can help define your life's purpose.

Objective To explore in a group setting the elements which provide real passion in your life and discern patterns for harnessing this passion by identifying your life's purpose.

Instructions

1. The class should break up into three groups and select a leader and a recorder. The leader will make certain everyone participates fully and completes the task in a timely way. The recorder will take careful notes and summarize the content of the discussion for the other groups.

2. Each member of the group writes down elements in their life that evoke great passion in their lives. Some examples are:

acting	religion	social issues
student politics	writing	injustice
rock music	children/family	the homeless

3. After each member of the group has identified their element of passion, they will briefly describe how this passion manifests itself in their life. As each person relates their passion, the group should look for patterns of passionate behavior. As patterns of passionate behavior are identified, the group members will try to define the role passion has played in their life and how this passion can lead to an understanding of the purpose of their life.

4. After each group has completed this discussion, the leader should summarize the patterns and generalities they discovered for the other groups.

Concluding Remarks

The world has many examples of how passion has defined great men and women: Joan of Arc for her country and religion and Mozart for his music. Will Keim invites you to discern those things in your life about which you are passionate and to pursue them. This passion is where you find your life's purpose. After you complete this activity, ask yourself the following questions:

a. Are you a passionate person? If so, why; and if not, why not?
b. What can your passion in life tell you about your purpose?
c. What is it that you want to spend the rest of your life doing?

Lesson 5 Purpose

How Personal Qualities Can Define Purpose

Purpose To state what personal qualities are most important in your life.

Objective With one other person, to answer questions which will help you identify the personal qualities which are most important in your life and which will help you clarify your purpose.

Instructions

1. Select a partner you can trust. A member of your class would be best, but a close friend or your roommate will be fine.

2. Sit in a comfortable chairs facing each other. Maintain eye contact.

3. You will ask your partner the following four questions, five times each, with your partner responding as quickly as possible. Write down your answers each time. The questions are:

I will trust my feelings because...

I will follow my heart because...

I will find something to do and do it well because...

I will do it so well that someone will pay me to do it because...

An example of answers would be:

I will trust my feeling because they are a window into my intuition.
I will trust my feelings because they have saved me from pain in the past.
I will trust my feelings because without them, life would be shallow and barren.
I will trust my feelings because they have the power to lead me to great joy and passion for my life's work.

4. After you have completed all four questions five times each, switch roles and ask your partner the four questions as rapidly as possible.

5. Once you have completed this exercise, review your answers and see what personal qualities come from them.

Discuss with your partner the qualities you value and how these qualities can help you clarify your life's purpose.

Concluding Remarks

Our culture seems to celebrate superficial things like material possessions, and physical appearance. Yet our heroes continue to be people such as Mahatma Gandhi, John F. Kennedy, Martin Luther King, and Mother Theresa. No wonder it's so difficult to discern our real purpose in American society. After you have completed this activity, ask yourself the following questions:

a. What kind of a person do you want to be?
b. What actions and behaviors give you real joy?
c. What are the things that you are really passionate about?
d. How will your life serve others?

JOURNAL ENTRY ON PURPOSE

You are about to write your own retirement speech. Project your life into the future. You have lived a long and productive life. Write what you want to be remembered for by your friends, family and professional colleagues. What qualities will you possess? What will be your greatest achievements? What legacy will you pass on to your children? What would you perceive to be the greatest compliment you could bestow upon yourself? After you have written this speech, write an action plan to accomplish these achievements or to attain these qualities.

RESOURCES

Fulghum, R. (1989). <u>All I Really Need to Know I Learned in Kindergarten: Uncommon Thoughts on Common Things</u>. New York: Villard Books.

Merwin, S. J. (1991). <u>Real Self: The Inner Journey of Courage</u>. Minnetonka, MN: Tiger Lily Press.

Robbins, A. (1991). <u>Awaken The Great Within</u>. New York: Simon & Schuster.

Sinetar, M. (1987). <u>Do What You Love, The Money Will Follow: Discovering Your Right Livelihood</u>. New York: Dell Publishing, Bantam, Double Day, Dell Publishing Group.

LESSON 6

YOURSELF

WHO AM I?

Purpose To discover different aspects of who you are.

Objectives To identify different aspects of who you are through objects that you carry with you every day and to discover through these objects how you are similar and different from other students in the class.

Instructions

1. Think about the following question—"Who am I?"

2. From your wallet or purse, pockets, or anything else you are carrying with you, select three things that help answer the question—"Who am I?"

3. Go around the room and share what three objects you selected and explain why they help provide insights into who you are.

4. Answer the following questions:

How were the objects that you selected <u>similar</u> to those selected by other members of the class?

How were they <u>different</u>?

Lesson 6 Yourself

Concluding Remarks

We often carry objects that are important to us for a variety of different reasons. These objects are often representations of who we are as individuals—lover of music, sports fan, traveler—and of the roles that we play—friend, brother, student. After you complete this activity, ask yourself the following questions:

a. In the past, have you carried with you things that were especially important to you? What were they? What did they represent? How did they help answer the question "Who am I?"
b. Why do you think you carry these things? Would they mean as much to you if you left them at home?

COLLAGE

Purpose To creatively portray different aspects of who you are through images and words.

Objectives To express your creativity and visually show who you are through various images and words.

Supplies Large piece of poster board, magazines, scissors, glue

Time Approximately 45—60 minutes

Instructions

1. A collage is a collection of images and words that relate to a specific theme. Cut out pictures and words from magazines, newspapers or other print media that describe you, show qualities you possess, or identify roles that you play.

2. Glue the pictures and words to the poster board in some grouping or order that makes sense to you.

3. Show your collage to the rest of the class. Tell the class why you chose the pictures and words in your collage. Tell them also why you grouped or ordered the pictures the way you did. Note: You could do this exercise at the beginning of the term and again at the end. It can be interesting to note how you've changed.

Concluding Remarks

The arts provide us with another way to show who we are. Collages can be a powerful tool in this process. Once finished, your project can be laminated for greater permanence. It's really fun to save your collages and look back on them several years later. You'll be amazed at how you are similar and different from the person who created it years before. After you complete this activity, ask yourself the following questions:

a. Did you have a difficult time trying to find pictures that represented certain aspects of yourself? Why or why not?
b. Did other people in your class choose different ways to express he same qualities that you have? How were the ways of expression different? Why do you think you all chose different ways to express this quality?

Journal Assignment—Yourself

If you were asked to create a musical collage, what songs would you include? How about a collage of television shows—what would be included? Which movies would you use to describe your life? What works of literature? Write a journal entry listing a couple songs, television shows, movies, books, or other mass media that could be used to describe your life. Why did you choose these particular works?

RESOURCES

Bach, R. (1984). <u>The Bridge Across Forever</u>. New York: Dell.

Bloomfield, H., Vettese, S., and Kory, R. (1989). <u>Lifemates</u>. New York: Signet.

Bridges, W. (1980). <u>Transitions</u>. Reading, MA: Addison-Wesley.

Bridges, W. (1991). <u>Managing Transitions</u>. Reading, MA: Addison-Wesley.

Brooks, S. (1990). <u>The Art of Good Living</u>. Boston: Houghton Mifflin.

Buber, M. (1958). <u>I and Thou</u>. New York: Charles Scribner's Sons.

Burns, D. (1985). <u>Intimate Connections</u>. New York: Signet.

Coleman, E. and Edwards, B. (1979). <u>Brief Encounters</u>. Garden City, NY: Anchor.

Colgrove, M., Bloomfield, H., & McWilliams, P. (1976). <u>How to Survive the Loss of a Love</u>. New York: Bantam.

Covey, S. (1989). <u>The 7 Habits of Highly Effective People</u>. New York: Simon and Schuster.

Cxikszentmiahalyi, M. (1990. <u>Flow</u>. New York: Harper & Row.

de Saint Exupery, A. (1943). <u>The Little Prince</u>. New York: Harcourt, Brace & World.

Gibran, K. (1975). <u>The Prophet</u>. New York: Alfred A. Knopf.

Keen, S. and Valley-Fox, A. (1989). <u>Your Mythic Journey</u>. Los Angeles: Jeremy P. Tarcher.

Myers, D. (1992). <u>The Pursuit of Happiness</u>. New York: Avon.

Powell, J. (198). <u>Why Am I Afraid to Tell You Who I Am?</u> Allen, TX: Tabor.

Powell, J. (1982). <u>Why Am I Afraid to Love?</u> Allen, TX: Tabor.

Powell, J. (1985). <u>Will the Real Me Please Stand Up?</u> Allen, TX: Tabor. (Communication focus)

LESSON 7

EDUCATION

WHY ATTEND COLLEGE?

Purpose To establish the objectives for obtaining a college education.

Objective In a group setting, to create a hierarchical list of the primary reasons for attending college.

Instructions

1. Divide into groups of 10 to 15 people. Each group should elect a leader and a recorder for the group. This leader will make certain the group process moves along smoothly throughout the exercise. If there is more than one group, the recorder will summarize the content (information) and process (method by which the content was obtained) of their group activity.

2. Each member of the group should write down the primary reason why they are attending college. The reasons can be a mix of practical, i.e. "to get a job," and philosophical, i.e. "to gain wisdom."

3. After each student has written their reason, the leader should conduct a group consensus task to rank-order all the reasons for attending college. The group should decide which reason is most important and second most important, etc. Each group must arrive at this list through discussion and reasoning and without averaging, "horse trading" (you vote for my first choice and I will vote for your choice), or "majority rule" voting.

4. Once each group has completed this task, the recorder of each group should present a report on the process and results of their consensus on the purpose of attending college.

Concluding Remarks

Everyone comes to college for different reasons. However the purpose of education, as Will Keim states, is fundamentally "the education of character...education will prove to be the way to a better self and ultimately to a way of improving everything you touch." After you complete this activity, ask yourself the following questions:

a. What are your goals for your college education?
b. Were you surprised by some of the other members of your group and their reasons for getting an education?
c. Have you gained some additional short-term and long-term goals from this exercise?

Lesson 7   Education

GETTING YOUR MONEY'S WORTH
OUT OF COLLEGE

Purpose To identify ways to maximize the educational experience of college.

Objective To brainstorm with a partner a strategy for maximizing the educational impact of college and its formation of your character.

Instructions 1. Pair up with a person you can trust. A member of your class would be best, but a friend or your roommate would be fine. Sit facing your partner in a comfortable chair. You may want to turn on music to relax.

2. You should have a discussion with your partner on the value of a college education. Try to give longer than one phrase or sentence reflections on the following topics and issues. Provide specific examples or suggestions on your reflections.

What does education mean to you?

How can you use college to enhance your educational process?

In practical terms what new behaviors or new habits do you want to acquire?

What extra curricular activities do you want to explore?

What workshops or courses do you want to take to help you change? (i.e. assertiveness training, substance abuse, writing skills, etc.)

What action plan will assist you in becoming the person you would like to become?

3. Reverse roles with your partner so that they can reflect on the meaning of education for them.

4. Each partner should briefly reflect on the answers his/her partner gave to the above questions. An example would be: "I'm not certain that you are as shy as you think you are." or "Writing for the college newspaper may help you realize your goal of becoming a journalist."

Concluding Remarks

As a consumer, you have the right and obligation to demand a fair return on your investment in a college education. You would not go to Europe and stay in your hotel room. So why would you not take full advantage of the opportunities college provides. After you have completed this activity, ask yourself the following questions:

a. How can I maximize my return on investment?
b. What skills or experiences do I want to broaden in college?
c. What action plan do I have to utilize my classes, faculty, extracurricular and social opportunities at college?

JOURNAL ENTRY ON EDUCATION

You may have come to college to get a good paying job or to find a partner for life. But the real importance of college is, as Will Keim says, "the education of character." What does it mean to you to be educated? What role does education play in the formation of your character? How are you going to maximize the educational process in your college experience? How will higher education assist in the "education of your character?"

Lesson 8

FINANCES

Creating a Financial Plan

Purpose To create a budget and be aware of how you choose to spend your money.

Objective To consciously allocate and spend your money on items you have indicated as priorities for yourself.

Instructions

1. Determine how much money you have at your discretion to spend each month. Include all sources of income: job, student loans, scholarships, etc.

2. Create a list of items on which you might need or want to spend money. This list could include items such as recreation, food, laundry, toiletries, clothes, gas, etc.

3. Determine how much of your money you will spend per month on each category and write that amount next to the item. Your total amount of expenditures must not exceed your monthly income.

4. During the first month, keep a log of all expenditures you make and at the end of the month, compare your budget with your actual expenditures. Do not forget to include your credit card purchases. If necessary, adapt your budget to reflect your actual spending patterns. If you are spending more than your income, decide in which areas you will cut back on your spending.

5. Continue to track your expenditures and compare actual spending with your budget at the end of each month.

Concluding Remarks For many students, financial resources are limited, so choices about when and how to spend money are quite important. By designing a budget that reflects your needs, you will be able to provide direction on how to spend your money as long as that budget accurately reflects your needs. As a tool, budgets can be changed whenever your needs change. Do not hesitate to alter your budget if your situation changes. Just remember that how you allocate and spend your money is up to you with the end goal being to not spend more money than you have available to you each month. After you complete this activity, ask yourself the following questions:

a. Was it difficult for you to create a budget for yourself? Why or why not?
b. Will it be difficult for you to stick with the budget you designed for yourself? Why or why not?
c. What ideas or suggestions could you brainstorm for yourself that might assist you in following your budget?
d. How could learning to work with a budget now be helpful to you in the future?

FINANCIAL AID EXPLORATION

Purpose   To better understand the financial obligations and resources available to you in financing your education.

Objective   To acquaint yourself with the financial aid office and the people who work there and to have your questions answered and reduce any stress you may have about assuming loans to finance your education.

Instructions

1. Schedule an appointment with a financial aid officer.

2. Before your appointment, generate a list of questions you want to ask about taking out a student loan. This list might include questions such as, "When will I have to start repaying my loan?" "How much money am I eligible to borrow each year?" "What happens to my loans if I decide I want to go on to graduate school?"

3. When you meet with the financial aid officer, explain that you are interested in better understanding the short and long term implications of financing your education and ask your questions!

Concluding Remarks

Many college students assist in financing their college education by securing student loans. While loans assist in reducing the immediate stress of paying for college, taking out a loan raises a number of questions for most students. By talking with someone from the financial aid office about the short and long term implications of student loans, you will get a greater understanding of your financial obligations. By understanding the fiscal expectations placed on you, you can deal with them effectively and reduce any stress you might be feeling regarding the financing of your education. After you complete this activity, ask yourself the following questions:

a. Do you now have a better understanding of your financial obligations?
b. What was it like to discuss your financial situation with a financial aid officer? What emotions did it evoke for you?
c. Did working through the financial questions you had about covering the cost of your education answer any other financial questions for you?
d. How can the process of finding answers to your financial aid questions apply to future financial situations you might envision for yourself?

JOURNAL ENTRY ON FINANCES

Invest in yourself. What does investing in yourself mean to you at this point in time? Five years from now? Ten years from now?

RESOURCES

Ellis, D.A. (1984). <u>Becoming a Master Student</u>. Rapid City, SD: College Survival, Inc. (Refer to Chapter 10).

Federal Student Aid Information Center
   1-(800)-433-3243

Financial Aid Office (See campus directory for location and telephone number.)

LESSON 9

CONSUMERISM

WHERE DO THE $$$ GO?

Purpose To discover the costs associated with various parts of the college experience.

Objectives To help you develop a heightened interest in how your tuition and fee money is spent by looking at the cost of operating college.

Supplies College catalogue or other source which lists the costs of various portions of your education.

Instructions

1. Collect the following university information: institutional budget with as detailed a breakdown of income and expenditures as possible; costs of attending college including tuition, room and board, and various fees. Try to get as complete a breakdown as possible. This may mean visiting several offices. If you are working in a group, you may divide up the tasks among group members.

2. Determine how much each hour of class is costing you. To do this, multiply the number of weeks in a term (usually from 12—16) by the number of hours of class you're taking each week. Divide this number into the cost of tuition for a term or semester. Remember that your tuition money also pays for things associated with instruction including the library, some student services, administrative functions, etc.

$$\text{Weeks in a Term} \times \text{Class Hours per Week} = \text{Total Number of Hours in Class per Term}$$

$$\frac{\text{Cost of Tuition}}{\text{Total Number of Hours in Class per Term}} = \text{Cost per Class Hour}$$

3. Determine how your student fee money is spent. This information is usually available from the student activities office.

Lesson 9 Consumerism

4. Determine how much of the institution's budget comes from state and federal sources and private donations. This information should be available from your institution's business or budget office.

5. Briefly answer the following questions:

How do you feel about how your money is spent?

How much does it "cost" you to skip a class? How do you feel about this?

Are you satisfied with how your student fees are spent? How could you change this process?

Were you surprised at the percentage of your education that was paid by state, federal, and private sources?

What is the best value for your dollar?

What is the worst value for your dollar?

Concluding Remarks

College is an expensive undertaking. By being a wise consumer, you may be prompted to use the many services and activities that are available to you on the campus. After all, you're paying for them. After you complete this activity, ask yourself the following questions:

a. In what ways can I cut my tuition expenses by not paying for things that I do not use?

b. In what ways can I get the most out of my tuition payments?

THE BUCK GOES HERE!

Purpose To visit various parts of the college campus which are financially supported by student tuition and fees.

Objectives To use a campus map to locate different parts of the campus which you support financially and to find out about programs and services that you might want to utilize now or at a later date.

Supplies A listing of various student services offices and campus map.

Instructions 1. Identify the different student services areas which exist on your campus. These will include the student health service, counseling center, student activities center, student union, etc. Try to get as complete a breakdown as possible. This may mean visiting several offices. Then find out the amount of the student fee you pay per term. Use the form below and fill in the blank lines with any areas and fees not specifically mentioned. If you are working in a group, you may divide up the tasks among group members.

Fee	Amount of student fee per term
Athletics	$
Counseling Center	$
Health Center	$
Student Activities	$
Student Union	$
_____	$
_____	$
_____	$
_____	$
_____	$
_____	$
Total Student Fees	$

Lesson 9 Consumerism

2. Visit each of these areas, noting programs and services that are available and hours of service. Pick up any interesting informational materials that are available.

3. Briefly answer in writing the following questions:

What did you learn about the programs and services that are available to you?

What programs and services might you be interested in using now or at a later date?

Concluding Remarks

Being a wise consumer means being aware of the many services and activities that are available to you on the campus. Some of them are very visible on the campus, others are hidden away. Almost all are staffed by people who are genuinely interested in making your college experience more successful. They are also committed to making college more interesting and entertaining. After you complete this activity, ask yourself the following questions:

a. Which of these services would you have found on your own without doing this activity?
b. How can you help to make students more aware of lesser-known services?

JOURNAL ENTRY ON CONSUMERISM

College is an expensive undertaking, no matter what school you are attending. In order to be a wise consumer, you need to be actively involved in getting the most out of your education and the programs and services that the institution provides. As your journal entry, discuss what could you do to get more out of your college experience.

RESOURCES

Consumer Reports magazine.

Consumer Digest magazine.

Annual "Best Values in College" issues of *U.S. News & World Report* or *Money* magazines.

Lesson 10

Parents

TO BE A PARENT...TO BE A CHILD

Purpose To gain insight into what it means to be a parent.

Objective To learn to see your world through your parent's eyes by role-playing what it is like to be your parent(s).

Instructions Pair up with a person you can trust. A member of your class would be best, but a friend or your roommate would be fine.

2. Your partner should role play you, while you become your same-sex parent (son will become father, daughter will become mother.) In these roles, discuss the following issues:

How does your parent feel about you?

What goals does you parent have for you and have they been met?

Is the parent pleased with your progress in college? Why or why not?

How would the parent feel if you moved home after graduation? Would it be seen as a failure, momentary setback or a necessity?

What is the one thing your parent is most pleased with about you?

How does your parent feel most misunderstood by you?

3. Reverse roles with your parent and have them act as their parent while you become the child.

Concluding Remarks This exercise will help you understand and appreciate your relationship with your same-sex parent. If time permits, you may want to repeat this exercise as your opposite-sex parent as well. After you complete this activity, ask yourself the following questions:

a. How is it to be your parent(s)?
b. What are the essential issues between you and your parent(s)?
c. Have you gained a better appreciation for your parent(s)?
d. How can you make your relationship with your parent(s) more harmonious?

MAKING PEACE

Purpose To make peace with your parents.

Objective To brainstorm with others strategies for making peace with your parents and affirming their basic goodness.

Instructions

1. Brainstorming is a process of developing new and creative ways of viewing an issue. In this exercise you will brainstorm ways of making peace with your parents. The major rule of brainstorming is that all ideas are valuable. It's the craziest idea which can lead to a breakthrough in changing your view on an issue. So it is imperative that all ideas are accepted by the group in a non-critical, non-judgmental way.

2. Divide the class into groups of eight to ten students. Each group should elect a leader and a recorder for the group. The leader will make certain the group process moves along smoothly through the brainstorming process and that all members of the group are participating. The recorder will take notes and summarize the group's results for the other groups.

3. Each member of the group should suggest several ways to make peace with their parents. The recorder of the group should write down each idea in a list that is easily seen by all group members. (This may be on a newspaper pad, a blackboard, or other piece of paper.) After no more than 30 minutes, these brainstorming sessions should be completed.

4. Once each group is done, the recorder of each group should summarize their results for the other groups.

Concluding Remarks

As a college student, some of you have left home. Some of you have painful lives at home, while others have primarily happy lives with their parents. In either case, it is important to make peace with your parents and affirm their basic goodness. As Will Keim states, "...never look back because you cannot change a thing except for those adjustments you make today." After you complete this activity, ask yourself the following questions:

a. Can you make peace with your parents?
b. Put yourself in their place and with their human imperfections. Can you still affirm their positive qualities?
c. Are there things you can do or say to your parents to help you let go of the past and move on to your future?

Journal Entry on Parents

Some of you have deep love and affection for your parents. Others may feel ambivalence or antipathy toward them. Maybe the major lessons that they taught you was not to be like them! Take some time to look at your parents as people and then as your parents. What do you consider your parent(s)' admirable qualities? What do you consider your parent(s)' unfavorable qualities? What have your parents taught you?

RESOURCES

Bloomfield, H. H., M.D. (1983). <u>Making Peace with Your Parents: The Key to Enriching Your Life and All Your Relationships</u>. New York: Ballantine Books.

LESSON 11

FRESHMAN

NEW ACTIVITY IDENTIFICATION

Purpose To identify a new activity that you are interested in learning or trying out.

Objective To create a plan of action for testing out a new interest, and hence have a greater incentive to put your interest in a new activity into action.

Supplies Your college catalogue.

Instructions

1. Take out your college catalogue and review the section on student clubs and organizations, campus activities, sports and recreational activities. Identify one new activity that is of interest to you that you would like to learn or test out.

2. Create a plan of action for testing out your interest in this new activity by answering the following questions:

a. Who is the contact person for the group?

b. How do you get in contact with that person?

c. Where/when does this activity meet?

d. How does a new person get involved in the group?

e. Does this new activity require anything such as special gear or equipment? If so, how do I rent or obtain these items?

f. When is the first opportunity available to me to test out my interest in this activity?

3. At the next possible opportunity, put your plan of action into motion by acting on the information you collected above.

Concluding Remarks College provides students with the opportunity to get involved in numerous activities that are thoroughly new experiences to them. Often, the "newness" of the experiences and a fear of failure can keep students from becoming involved in these activities. While this fear might seem to keep us "safe," what it really keeps us from is taking a risk that would most likely lead to personal growth and development. Hopefully, by collecting information and creating an action plan, you will feel empowered to take a risk and try something new that is of interest to you.

After you complete this activity, ask yourself the following questions:

a. Did exploring a new activity make you feel more interested in actually trying it out? Why or why not?
b. Does getting involved in an activity that is completely new to you cause you any anxieties? Can you identify what it is about the experience that triggers anxieties for you?
c. In the past, have you ever wanted to try something new but talked yourself out of it? What caused you to talk yourself out of participating in the activity?
d. In the past, how have you felt about yourself after you attempted something that was new to you?

"What I Have Learned As A New Student" Letter

Purpose To assist you in realizing that even though you are a 'freshman,' you are quickly adjusting and mastering your new environment.

Objective To write a letter that reflects on everything you have accomplished to date, and to tell others how you are making progress and succeeding.

Instructions Imagine that your college's freshmen orientation staff has asked you to write a letter that will be distributed to next year's freshmen class during their fall orientation. The staff wants you to write a letter entitled, "What I Have Learned as a New Student" which recounts all of the new experiences you have encountered and learned from thus far in your college career.

"What I Have Learned as a New Student"

Lesson 11 Freshman

Concluding Remarks

As a freshman, you are placed in a situation where almost everything is new to you. Because everything is new, you must learn how to quickly adapt and master the newness that surrounds you. Often, you fail to stop and recognize how successfully you are meeting the many demands placed on you. By asking you to spend a few minutes recounting all of the new situations you have faced and have successfully mastered in the past few weeks, it becomes obvious that you are adjusting to the college environment and that your knowledge about being a college student is expanding rapidly. By creating a "laundry list" of your successes, you will have even greater motivation for mastering future learning situations. After you complete this activity, ask yourself the following questions:

a. Were you surprised by the number of things you have learned already?
b. Was there anything on the list of items you have learned that surprised you? Why?
c. Does your list of things you have learned tell you anything about yourself?
d. How does writing down the things you have learned in the last few weeks make you feel about yourself?

JOURNAL ENTRY ON BEING A FRESHMAN

Describe a risk that you have taken recently. What did you learn about yourself from taking this risk?

RESOURCES

Ellis, D.A. (1984). <u>Becoming a Master Student</u>. Rapid City, SD: College Survival Inc.

Upcraft, M.L., & Gardner, J. (1989). <u>The Freshmen Year Experience: Helping Students Survive and Succeed in College</u>. San Francisco: Jossey-Bass.

You Can Survive your Freshmen Year Pamphlet (1994). Printed in USA by Channing L. Bete Co., Inc., 200 State Road, South Deerfield, MA 01373, 1-800-628-7733. When ordering, ask for item number 40816B-7-93.

LESSON 12

EXPERIENCE

Someday I'd Like To....

Purpose   To develop a wish list of things you'd like to do sometime in your life.

Objectives   To create a list of things you'd like to do sometime in your life and to have this list in collage form so that it can be referred to throughout your life.

Instructions
1. Think of all the things you'd like to do sometime in your life.

2. Write down a list of all of these things. Try to include as many experiences as possible and be as specific as you can.

3. Now take your list and bring it to life on a large piece of paper. You may cut out and glue pictures from magazines, write words with colorful markers, attach various objects of importance, etc. Be as creative as you can be. Try to make your collage/display represent you and your dreams.

4. Share your collage/display with the class. When all of you have shared your works, discuss the following questions:

How were the collages similar? How were they different?

Did any themes emerge from your collages/displays?

Concluding Remarks

From time to time, we'll read about someone who has had an experience that was taken from a list they developed early in life. Things like "see the Nile River" or "have a poem published in a literary magazine" or "become really, really rich" may seem very far away right now but are definitely within reach sometime in your life. Having a sense of what experiences you'd like to have is an important first step to actually having them. Save your list and collage/display. It will make interesting reading and viewing years from now. And you'll be able to check off all the things you've done. After you complete this activity, ask yourself the following questions:

a. What types of experiences did you primarily consider? Travel? Personal growth experiences? Experiences in your local area? Possessions to have or use? Spiritual experiences? Other types of experiences?

b. Why do your experiences appeal to you? What do they say about who you are?

THEM CHANGES

Purpose To recognize how you've changed since you first came to college.

Objectives To experience and show through skits how much you have changed since the first day of college.

Instructions 1. Remember the first day you arrived on campus? What were you thinking and feeling? Jot down a couple notes to yourself.

2. Now break up into small groups of three to five students. Develop a skit that shows what your various first days were like. Be creative and have fun.

3. Do your skit for the rest of the class.

4. Now think about the person you are today. Are you like the person you portrayed in your skit? How have you changed? What has been easy about these changes? What has been difficult? Draw something (a picture or image) that shows how you've changed from the person you were when you first arrived on campus to the person you are now.

5. Get back into your same small groups and discuss your drawings and discuss how each of the members of your group have changed.

Concluding Remarks

Change is hard, whether it's a big change or a little one. While change is hard, it is also inevitable. We can't grow and develop without changing. Often the things that excite us the most about a new experience are also the things that scare us the most. For example, we may be very excited about the possibility of meeting new people but we're also very scared that no one will like us in our new locations. The process of growth and development as people is one kind of change that can be particularly stressful. Realizing how far you've come already since you first arrived on campus can help show you how much you've learned already. After you complete this activity, ask yourself the following questions:

a. How have I made the changes that I have made since beginning college?
b. How has the recent changes in my life affected my life as a whole?
c. Have I been instrumental in helping anyone else make changes, either while beginning college or during any other change in his or her life?

JOURNAL ENTRY—EXPERIENCE

College is not always like you may have imagined it would be. Write a letter to a friend describing your college experience thus far. Specifically point out how it has been like you thought it would be and how it has been surprising or different.

RESOURCES

Bach, R. (1984). <u>The bridge across forever</u>. New York: Dell.

Bridges, W. (1980). <u>Transitions</u>. Reading, MA: Addison-Wesley.

Brooks, S. (1990). <u>The art of good living</u>. Boston: Houghton Mifflin.

Buber, M. (1958). <u>I and thou</u>. New York: Charles Scribner's Sons.

Burns, D. (1985). <u>Intimate connections</u>. New York: Signet.

Coleman, E. and Edwards, B. (1979). <u>Brief encounters</u>. Garden City, NY: Anchor.

Covey, S. (1989). <u>The 7 habits of highly effective people</u>. New York: Simon & Schuster.

Cxikszentmiahalyi, M. (1990. <u>Flow</u>. New York: Harper & Row.

de Saint Exupery, A. (1943). <u>The little prince</u>. New York: Harcourt, Brace & World.

Gibran, K. (1975). <u>The prophet</u>. New York: Alfred A. Knopf.

John-Roger & McWilliams, P. (1990). <u>Do it!</u> Los Angeles: Prelude.

Keen, S. and Valley-Fox, A. (1989). <u>Your mythic journey</u>. Los Angeles: Jeremy P. Tarcher.

Maclean, N. (1976). <u>A river runs through it</u>. Chicago: University of Chicago.

Myers, D. (1992). <u>The pursuit of happiness</u>. New York: Avon.

Olson, K. (1975). <u>Can you wait till Friday?</u> Greenwich, CT: Fawcett.

Peck, M. (1987). <u>The different drum</u>. New York: Simon and Schuster.

Peck, M. (1992). <u>A world waiting to be born</u>. New York: Bantam.

Powell, J. (198). <u>Why am I afraid to tell you who I am?</u> Allen, TX: Tabor.

Powell, J. (1982). <u>Why am I afraid to love?</u> Allen, TX: Tabor.

Powell, J. (1985). <u>Will the real me please stand up?</u> Allen, TX: Tabor. (Communication focus)

Schlossberg, N. (1990). Marginality and mattering: Key issues in building community. In D. Roberts, *Designing campus activities to foster a sense of community*, New Directions for Student Services, #48, 5-15.

LESSON 13
ATTENDANCE

Faculty/Student Role Reversal

Purpose To make you reflect on the importance of attending class.

Objective To articulate the importance of attending class as if you were the professor and to gain a new appreciation for attending class.

Instructions

1. Pretend you are a faculty member and are talking to one of your students who has not been attending your class. List five reasons you would share with this student as to why it is important for him/her to attend your class.

As a faculty member, I feel it is important for you to attend my class because...

1.

2.

3.

4.

5.

2. Take the five responses you listed above from your 'faculty member' point of view and rewrite them below, this time from your point of view as a student.

As a student, it is important for me to attend class because...

1.

2.

3.

4.

5.

Concluding Remarks

Often, when an person is asked to view a situation from another's point of view, an understanding is created that did not exist previously. By asking you to place yourself into your faculty member's point of view in regards to the importance of attending class, you now have a much clearer understanding of how and why class attendance is related to your academic success. By understanding the issue of class attendance from both a faculty member's and a student's point of view, your motivation for attending class will hopefully be increased. After you complete this activity, ask yourself the following questions:

a. What was it like to think about attending class from a faculty member's point of view?
b. Did the importance of attending class change when you listed the reasons from your point of view as a student?
c. Do you think faculty members and students have different reasons as to why they believe attending class is important? Why or why not?

I Want to be in College Because...

Purpose To identify the reasons you chose to attend college and understand how the reasons for being in college relate to attending class.

Objective There are many possible reasons for why you have chosen to attend college. By asking you to list these reasons, you will articulate for yourself why you have made this decision. Once you know why you are on campus, you can begin to reflect on how attendance in your classes relates to your academic success and accomplishing your goals for being in college.

Instructions 1. Listed below is a sentence stem that reads, "I want to be in college because..." After thinking about why you want to be in college, complete the sentence stem by listing all of your reasons.

I want to be in college because...

2. Review each reason you listed and determine how many of your reasons for being in college require you to attend class if you hope to have a successfully large return on your investments of time and money.

Concluding Remarks Attendance in class is vitally important if you are to be successful in your academic pursuits. By identifying your goals and acknowledging that meeting these goals is largely dependent on your attendance in class, you will hopefully have an even greater ownership in attending your classes. After you complete this activity, ask yourself the following questions:

a. Did you list any reason for wanting to be in college that you had not previously considered? If so, what do you think influenced you to list this new reason for wanting to be in college?

b. If one of your faculty members asked you to explain the relationship between attending class and meeting your goals, what would your response be?

c. What might be the possible consequences of your not attending your classes? How would you feel about those consequences?

JOURNAL ENTRY ON ATTENDANCE

College requires an investment from you in terms of time and money. How valuable do you feel your time and money are to you at this point in your life? How does your investment of time and money relate to your attending or not attending class? How will you justify investing your time and money in a college education if you choose to not attend class?

Lesson 13 Attendance

RESOURCES

Ellis, D.A. (1984). <u>Becoming a Master Student</u>. Rapid City, SD: College Survival Inc.

LESSON 14
STUDYING

YOU TOO CAN BE AN EINSTEIN

Purpose To develop new study habits.

Objective With a partner, you will explore new study habits to increase your academic performance.

Instructions 1. Pair up with a person you can trust. A class member would be best, but a friend or your roommate would be fine, too.

2. Go back and forth 10 times each, asking each other to complete the following sentence 10 times each as rapidly as possible as you quickly complete it. The sentence is:

If I were an expert on study skills, I would...

Each time the sentence is said by your partner, you will try to come up with a new study skill. An example of this sentence completion would be:

a. Make "to do" lists and prioritize the items each night.
b. Write an outline for each paper.
c. Use a portable tape recorder to summarize a chapter in a textbook.
d. Take a writing workshop offered by the academic support department.

3. Once you have provided twenty sentence completions for this exercise (10 each), you and your partner should briefly discuss some new approaches to studying which this exercise has suggested to you.

Concluding Remarks As college students, you spend enormous amounts of time studying. However, you seldom spend enough time reflecting on the process of studying. Just a few minutes of this reflection can increase the effectiveness of the dozens of hours of studying. Periodically, review the process by which you study and see if there are simple ways that it can be improved. After you complete this activity, ask yourself the following questions:

a. How can I improve my study skills?
b. What resources exist on campus to improve my study skills?
c. What suggestions did my partner provide concerning improving my study skills that I should investigate?

BRAINSTORMING TO BETTER STUDY SKILLS

Purpose To increase your knowledge of successful study habits.

Objective To brainstorm, in a group setting, better methods of studying.

Time This exercise should take 45-60 minutes depending on the size of the group.

Instructions

1. Brainstorming is a process of developing new and creative ways of solving a problem. In this exercise, in a group setting, you will brainstorm better, more effective ways of studying. The major rule of brainstorming is that all ideas are valuable. It's the craziest idea which can lead to a breakthrough in solving a problem. So it is imperative that all ideas are accepted by the group in a non-critical, non-judgmental way.

2. Divide into groups of eight to ten students. Each group should elect a chairperson or leader. This person will make certain the group process moves along smoothly through the brainstorming process and that everyone is contributing. In addition, if there is more than one group, the leader will summarize the group results of the brain storming session to the other groups.

3. The leader of the group should record each idea about how to improve the effectiveness of studying. Make certain that no one individual monopolizes the brainstorming process. Each member of the group should be given an opportunity to suggest several ways to improve student study skills.

4. After 30 minutes, these brainstorming sessions should be completed. Once each group has completed this task, the leader of each group should summarize the results of the brainstorming session to the other groups.

Concluding Remarks

Every student has at least a few study habits that have contributed to his or her academic success. The purpose of this exercise is to expand your repertoire of successful study habits. After you complete this activity, ask yourself the following questions:

a. What new study skills have I gained from this exercise?
b. Which of my own study skills were mentioned in other groups?
c. What new insights have I gained about studying?

Journal Activity on Studying

For one week keep a record on the form on the next page of all your study activities each day. Note the time and length of each activity and where you were studying. (Photocopy additional pages as necessary.) As you complete a study activity, give it a grade:

> A for very productive
> B for productive
> C for somewhat productive
> D for occasionally productive
> F for not productive at all

At the end of the week, review your journal entries. See if you can discern patterns where you are most and least productive in your studying. When are you most and least productive? In the morning? At night? What length of study time are you most productive - 1 hour? 2 hours? Where were you studying when you were most and least productive?

Based on this analysis, develop a written action plan to maximize your study strengths and summarize your study weaknesses.

Action Plan: (form on next page)

What I studied	Time of day	Duration	Where I studied	Grade

RESOURCES

McWhorter, K. T. (1995). <u>Study and Thinking Skills in College, third edition</u>. New York: Harper Collins Publishers.

Pauk, W. (1993). <u>How to Study in College, fifth edition</u>. Boston: Houghton Mifflin Company.

Lesson 15

MAJOR

CHARACTERISTICS I WILL LOOK FOR IN CHOOSING A MAJOR

Purpose To assist you in identifying characteristics that are important to you in choosing a major.

Objective By identifying characteristics that are of great personal value to you, you will be able to provide yourself with important direction in selecting a major that fits with your needs and goals.

Instructions 1. Listed below are ten phrases that describe opposite characteristics. Read each phrase and select the preference that best describes your attitudes and working style.

a. I prefer to work independently or I prefer to work in a group.

b. I prefer talking about theory or I prefer practical application of material.

c. I prefer classes that focus on logical analysis or I prefer classes that focus on personal interpretation.

d. I prefer watching/listening or I prefer doing.

e. I prefer relying on intuition or I prefer relying on logic.

f. I prefer using my imagination or I prefer using facts and data.

g. I prefer planning or I prefer action.

h. I prefer task-oriented assignments or I prefer people-oriented assignments.

i. I prefer to be idealistic or I prefer to be practical.

j. I prefer to take risks or I prefer to avoid taking risks.

2. Different majors have different characteristics. Think about the different majors offered at your institution and their characteristics. Compare your responses above with the characteristics of several majors that you would be interested in pursuing.

3. Based on your responses to questions 1 and 2, decide which types of majors would best suit your attitudes and working style.

Concluding Remarks

Academic disciplines differ on many levels including the types of skills and abilities they require of their students to be successful. By being aware of your values and attitudes, you can use these items as a measuring stick for choosing a major. For example, if you prefer to work in groups and interpret your information subjectively, you can test out different majors using these items as criteria. Majors that include these values as part of their course work will be a much better match for you than majors that do not include these preferences in the course work. After you complete this activity, ask yourself the following questions:

a. Based on the ten characteristics you selected above that describe your preferences, what did you learn about yourself?
b. Were you surprised or puzzled by any of the preference choices you made above? If so, what surprised or puzzled you?
c. What do your preferences say about you?
d. How will you use the information about your preferences to assist you in choosing an academic major?

MAKING MY DREAMS COME TRUE

Purpose To identify your dreams and consider how your choice of a major can help make your dreams a reality.

Objective Dreams are images of a future we envision for ourselves and whether we make those dreams a reality depends on the actions we take today. By listing your dreams, you will have a vivid picture of what you want for your future. By then reflecting on how your choice of a major can assist you in making those dreams a reality, you will be aware of an action step that can assist you in achieving your dreams.

Instructions Respond to the two sentence stems listed below:

I dream myself becoming...

My major will assist me in making my dreams come true by...

Concluding Remarks The decisions you make in life directly influence what path you will take. If you spend time reflecting on how a particular decision will impact your life, you will be able to choose the path that best suits your needs and goals. If you make a decision without reflecting on how it impacts your future, you often start down a path that will not take you where you most want to go. By beginning now to reflect on how your choice of a major will help you accomplish your future goals, you can be very intentional in starting yourself down the path that you choose to go down and explore. After you complete this activity, ask yourself the following questions:

a.   How did it feel to be asked to relate something very concrete like the choice of a major with your future dreams, which are much more abstract?
b.   Was thinking about your choice of an academic major and how it relates to your future dreams an easy connection for you to make?
c.   What did you learn from completing this activity?
d.   How will you apply this information to your selection of future course work?

JOURNAL ENTRY ON CHOOSING A MAJOR

When you were a child and people asked you what you wanted to be when you grew up, what did you tell them? Reflect on the different occupations you wanted to have as a child and identify what it was about each one that most intrigued you. Do the things about each occupation that intrigued you have anything in common? How do these commonalities relate to your choosing a major?

RESOURCES

Academic Advising Office (See campus directory for location and telephone number.)

Boldt, L. (1993). Zen and the Art of Making a Living. New York: Penguin Books.

Campbell Interest Inventory, Distributed by Consulting Psychologist Press, Inc., 557 College Avenue, Palo Alto, CA 94306.

Career Center (See campus directory for location and telephone number.)

Kolb's Learning-Style Inventory, McBer and Company, 137 Newbury Street, Boston, MA 02116, (617)-437-7080.

Opportunities In Series. VGM Career Horizons (a division of NTC Publishing Group). Lincolnwood, IL.

LESSON 16

STRESS

STRESS RELIEF
OR
HAPPINESS IS...

Purpose To develop quick, effective methods for reducing stress in your life.

Objective You will learn ways to relieve stress that can be utilized on a daily basis. At particularly stressful times, such as during exams or interpersonal conflicts, these methods can be used to provide immediate relief. Daily use of these methods can appreciably reduce the overall level of stress in your life thus improving your entire physiology.

Supplies A comfortable chair and a source of calming music.

Instructions

1. Dress casually in your favorite comfortable clothes. Sit in a comfortable chair with your feet on the floor and your arms resting on the arms of the chair.

2. Turn on the music. The music should be calm and soothing. Any of the "New Age" music, or recordings of whales, birds, or the surf will do. You may find the soundtrack from the movie "The Chariots of Fire" a little bit more upbeat and inspiring.

3. Sit up straight in the chair, close your eyes and relax.

4. Slowly breathe in and out. Breathe deeply from your diaphragm. Stress tends to promote shallow breathing, thus robbing your body of oxygen, a needed component of metabolism.

5. Next, you need to tense all of the muscles in your face as hard as you can and then relax. Repeat this process several times. Slowly work your way down your body alternating tensing and relaxing each area. Do your hands, arms, shoulders, chest, stomach, buttocks, thighs, calves, and finally your feet.

6. Now, with your eyes closed as you continue to breathe deeply, think back upon the happiest moment in your life. Make believe you are watching a slow motion videotape of this moment. Don't leave any details out. Is it inside or outside? What color are the walls or the sky? Who is there with you? What's the weather like? What sounds do you hear and what smells do you smell? Paint a picture in your mind. Concentrate

on all the small details, the grains of sand on the beach or the dust bunnies in the corner of the room.

7. Reflect upon how you felt at that time. Try to recreate those feelings now in your mind. Feel that joy and happiness once more; wallow in those feelings for a few minutes.

8. Once again, tense and relax the various parts of your body, beginning with your feet and ending with your hands. Then smile and frown several times. Hold the smile for a few minutes as you open your eyes and slowly come back to the present. Hear the music and concentrate on the details of the room. Wait a few minutes before beginning your normal activities. Feel the new found peace and relaxation.

Concluding Remarks

After this exercise you should feel much more relaxed than when you went into it. Stressful moments will pass and more joyful and happy ones will return.

Life is a series of ups and downs. As you become more at ease with who you are and how you feel, your stressful times will be seen as temporary and fleeting. If you find yourself stressed in class or before a presentation, just close your eyes and do a mini-exercise. Breathe deeply and tense and relax your entire body, particularly your facial muscles. Remember that at first you may feel awkward in this exercise, but as you do it every day for 15-20 minutes, it will become a natural stress-relieving daily process. After you complete this activity, ask yourself the following questions:

a. At what times do I feel most stressed?
b. How can I make the time to do things to help relieve stress when I am at my most stressful?

REDUCING STRESS

Purpose   To collaborate on identifying the causes of stress and ways to reduce it.

Objective   In a group setting, you will identify the major causes of stress in student life and develop an action plan to reduce it.

Time   This exercise should range from 45 - 60 minutes depending on the size of the group.

Instructions

1. Go to the blackboard or write on a sheet of paper one to three major sources of stress in your life.

2. Pool all of the responses in the class together. There should be 15-30 different sources of stress on the list.

3. As a group determine if some of the sources of stress can be grouped together into more general issues. A typical list might be:

Time Management
Over Commitment
Interpersonal Conflict
Disorganization
Test Anxiety
Family or Personal Problems

The group should come up with five to ten larger issues to address.

4. The class should break into groups for each issue based on the applicability of it to each member. Each group should elect or appoint a chairperson and a recorder.

5. The groups chairperson should lead a discussion on ways to reduce the stress caused by the issue. Each student should be encouraged to speak out on the issue. The recorder should take careful notes on the action plan to reduce stress surrounding their issue. The action plan should be as specific as possible.

6. After 20 minutes, reconvene the class. Each recorder will stand and summarize their action plan for reducing stress surrounding their issue. Other students can take notes on the various suggestions for reducing stress.

Lesson 16   Stress

Concluding Remarks

Life can be very stressful. Not all stressful situations can be avoided. However, much of the stress in college life comes from general issues of personal organization and interpersonal effectiveness. This exercise has given you the tools to continue the process of reducing stress in your life. You will be surprised how similar everyone's stressful situations are and how helpful the action plans can be. After you complete this activity, ask yourself the following questions:

a. Where does your stress come from? Faulty interpersonal skills? Faulty organizational skills?
b. Can skill development help you reduce or manage your stress more effectively?
c. What one new skill or behavior would reduce your stress substantially?
d. How can other students help you to reduce stress rather than trying to solve it alone?

JOURNAL ACTIVITY ON STRESS

List 25 things that "stress you out." If you have difficulty coming up with a list, keep a record of all the things that are stressful in the next few days or week. Once you have developed this list, prioritize the items on the list. Which item is the most stressful? Which item is the second most stressful? Continue through your list until all the items are prioritized. Many stressful situations derive from common problems in your life. Do you see patterns in what makes you more stressful? Are you chronically late? Are you a spendthrift? Do you over-commit too often? No life is free of stress, but a more organized lifestyle can reduce stress to more manageable levels. Once you see patterns of common problems in your life, you can then anticipate the problems and take steps to avoid it happening again. What actions will you take to avoid or alleviate this problem the next time?

RESOURCES

Borysenko, J., Ph.D. (1987) <u>Minding the Body, Mending the Mind</u>. Reading, MA: Addison-Wesley Publishing Co.

Davis, M., Ph.D., Eshelman, E. R., MSW, and McKay, M., Ph.D. (1980). <u>The Relaxation and Stress Reduction Workbook</u>. New Harbinger Publications, Inc.

LESSON 17

ALCOHOL

ALTERNATIVE ACTIVITIES TO ALCOHOL LIST

Purpose To identify the many alternative activities available to you on campus that do not involve alcohol.

Objective To brainstorm a list of alternative activities that do not involve drinking alcohol so that you will know that if you choose to drink alcohol, it is because you made an active choice to drink and not because it is the only social opportunity available to you.

Supplies College catalogue and local telephone book.

Instructions 1. For the next five minutes, brainstorm a list of activities that you would enjoy which do not include alcohol. These activities could range from active sports events to visiting a museum and everything in between--anything in which you would enjoy participating.

Activities That I Would Enjoy

2. After you complete your list, locate your college catalogue and put a check next to each activity that is available to you on campus. If an activity is not available on campus, check the local telephone book and determine if the activity is available to you through the community. Also, if you discover any activities that you were not familiar with that sound interesting, please add them to your list.

3. Make a copy of the activities that are available to you and post it in a visible place in your room. Add any additional information to the list that would be helpful to you such as telephone numbers or hours. This information will then be

available and helpful the next time you are trying to decide how to spend your time.

Concluding Remarks

If you choose to drink alcohol because you feel that there is nothing else available for you to do socially, you have not yet explored your options. By identifying what it is you enjoy and researching the availability of these activities on your campus, you will provide yourself with more diversity in your social life choices. Once this information is known to you, your choosing to drink or not drink will become just that--a choice-- and not something you feel you need to participate in solely because you have no other options. After you complete this activity, ask yourself the following questions:

a. Were you surprised by the number of social activities available on your campus? Did any of the activities offered seem especially interesting to you?
b. How likely are you to take advantage of these activities? Why or why not?
c. How do you feel about having this variety of non-alcoholic social opportunities available to you?

ALCOHOL AWARENESS WEEK
PROGRAM PLANNING

Purpose To identify the questions you would like to have answered regarding alcohol.

Objective To imagine yourself as a member of a committee planning an alcohol education series, identify questions and concerns that are relevant to you regarding alcohol, and increase your knowledge about alcohol by then finding answers to your questions.

Instructions 1. Imagine that you are a member of your campus' alcohol awareness committee and that as a group, you are planning the schedule of activities for alcohol awareness week. Your goal is to decide on three activities for the week that you think will a). provide important information to students regarding the use of alcohol, and b). be of interest to them. As a member of the committee, you were instructed at your last meeting to come prepared to the next meeting with two educational programming ideas. List two ideas below and include the type of information you would most like to see included in these programs.

Program Idea #1:_____

Information to be included or questions to be answered:

Program Idea #2:_____

Information to be included or questions to be answered:

2. Share your two ideas with your resident advisor or student activities director and ask him/her to consider using them to plan a program for your living group or your campus. You might also volunteer to assist in coordinating the program.

Concluding Remarks

The type of programs that you brainstormed most likely reflect the questions you have about alcohol or the information that you most want to know about alcohol. It is likely that your friends have many of the same questions about alcohol that you do. By passing on this information to someone like your resident advisor or student activities director, it will be possible to schedule an educational program that can serve to answer these questions. By having as much information as possible about alcohol, you will be able to make more informed decisions about using or not using alcohol. After you complete this activity, ask yourself the following questions:

a. Were you able to imagine yourself as a member of an alcohol education committee? Why or why not?
b. What do the program ideas you brainstormed suggest to you about your alcohol awareness level?
c. What might be the consequences of drinking alcohol without understanding as much as possible about it?

Lesson 17 Alcohol

JOURNAL ENTRY ON ALCOHOL

What decisions have you made about using or not using alcohol? How will you avoid pressure from others to keep you from altering the choices you have made for yourself regarding the use of alcohol?

RESOURCES

Alcohol Anonymous
(See local White Pages of telephone directory)

Al-Anon Family Group (Support program for family and friends of alcoholics)
(See local telephone directory)

Alcohol and Drug Abuse Education Program
U.S. Office of Education
400 Maryland Avenue, SW
Washington, D.C. 20702

American College Health Association
1300 Piccard Drive, Suite 200
Rockville, MD 20850
(301) 963-1100

BACCHUS of the US, Inc.
P.O. Box 100430
Denver, CO 80210
(303) 871-3068
(303) 871-2013 (FAX)

GAMMA
(Greeks Advocating Mature Management of Alcohol)
P.O. Box 100430
Denver, CO 80250-0430
(303) 871-3068
(303) 871-2013 (FAX)

The Johnson Institute (Provides references to appropriate agencies in your area)
7151 Metro Blvd. #250
Minneapolis, MN 55439-2122
1-(800)-231-5165 (US)
1-(800)-247-0484 (MN)

National Clearinghouse for Alcohol Information
P.O. Box 2345, Dept. #10
Rockville, MD 20852

National Council on Alcoholism
(202) 986-4433

TIPS (Training for Intervention Procedures by Servers of Alcohol)
Health Communications, Inc.
600 New Hampshire Avenue NW Suite 100
Washington, D.C. 20037
(202) 333-8267

Wisconsin Clearinghouse
P.O. Box 1468
Madison, WI 53701
(608) 263-2797

LESSON 18
DRUGS

PRO AND CON LIST OF USING DRUGS

Purpose To look at the pros and cons of drug use and how drugs can affect your life.

Objective To create a list of pros and cons of drug use. Then analyze the short- and long-term effects of each of these pros and cons to get a more comprehensive understanding of the effects of drug use.

Instructions 1. Create a list of pro and con reasons for using drugs. This list can be based on personal experience, the experience of people you know, or things that you have read.

PROS for using drugs	**CONS for using drugs**

2. Review each pro and con reason you listed above and explain how using drugs could affect you in the a) short term (1-4 years) and b) long term (5-10 years).

Concluding Remarks In order to make an informed decision, it is important to fully understand both sides of an issue. However, when drugs are the issue it is also vital to understand the effect that these substances can have on your life in both the short and long term. By identifying possible consequences that accompany the choice to use drugs, you will begin to understand the magnitude of this decision on your life. You can then make an informed choice on what you want your future to be by the choices you make regarding drugs. After you complete this activity, ask yourself the following questions:

a.   Was it difficult to list both the pros and cons for drug use?
b.   Which side of the argument was more difficult for you to list? Why?
c.   Could you argue the reasons on either side of your list equally well? Why or why not?
d.   Was it difficult to identify the possible effects that drug use could have on your life in the short term? In the long term?
e.   How does the pro/con list and the possible effects apply to your life at this present time?

STUDENT NEWSPAPER ARTICLE

Purpose To write an article on drug use that would have an educational impact on your peers.

Objective Peers have great influence on each other and can be very effective in teaching each other information on important issues. When involved in educating each other on the hazards of drug use, peers have the ability to make a significant difference in each others' lives. By writing an article for the student newspaper, you will have the opportunity to communicate with your peers on an important issue and hopefully, make an impact on your community.

Instructions Write a short column for your student newspaper on the hazards of drug use. State your main idea in the first paragraph, then back up that idea with two or three factual reasons. Please include information that you feel would be of greatest interest to your peers.

Concluding Remarks

In order to teach, you must first learn the information yourself. By writing an article for your peers on the hazards of drug use, you will have to begin by reflecting on this issue yourself, researching the information to answer your questions and then writing about this issue in an informative and convincing manner. Hopefully, by becoming a teacher on the hazards of drug use, you will also become an excellent learner. After you complete this activity, ask yourself the following questions:

a. Was it difficult for you to write a convincing article on the hazards of drug use? Why or why not?

b. Would it have been easier to write an article if your target audience was not your peers? Why or why not?

c. Would you consider actually submitting your article to the student newspaper? Why or why not?

d. How did the points you made in your article personally apply to your life?

JOURNAL ENTRY ON DRUGS

How can you be part of the solution and not part of the problem regarding the use of drugs in your living group? On your campus? In your community?

RESOURCES

Alcohol and Drug Abuse Education Program (Information on education and treatment materials)
U.S. Office of Education
400 Maryland Avenue, SW
Washington, D.C. 20702

Cocaine Hotline
1-(800)-COCAINE (262-2463)

Hazeldon Foundation (World's largest source of educational materials on chemical dependency)
Box 176
Center City, MN 55012-0176
1-(800)-328-9000 (US)
1-(800)-257-0070 (MN)

The Johnson Institute (Provides references to appropriate agencies in your area)
7151 Metro Blvd. #250
Minneapolis, MN 55439-2122
1-(800)-231-5165 (US)
1-(800)-247-0484 (MN)

Narcotics Anonymous
(See local White Pages of telephone directory)

Nar-Anon Family Group (Support group for family and friends of narcotic users)
(Use local telephone directory)

NIDA (National Institute on Drug Abuse)
1-(800)-662-4357

LESSON 19
SEX

QUESTIONS, QUESTIONS, AND MORE QUESTIONS

Purpose To learn more about sexual issues through discussions with your peers.

Objectives To provide an opportunity for you to ask questions about sexuality without fear of embarrassment, to provide a safe environment in which you can discuss important issues relating to sexuality and to provide an opportunity for you to share your attitudes and beliefs about sexuality with each other.

Supplies 3 X 5 notecards or slips of paper and pens or pencils
two containers of some type

Time The exercise can range from 15 minutes to over an hour depending on how many questions are posed to the group.

Instructions 1. On a slip of paper or notecard, write down a question you've always wanted to ask members of the opposite sex. Questions may address topics of sex, sexuality, dating, or other matters. Don't put your name on the slips so that questions will be anonymous. Put an F on the slip if you're a female and a M if you're a male. This will help keep the questions separate.

2. Collect the questions by gender. Have all the males put their questions into one container and all the females put their questions into another, separate container.

3. Divide the class with women on one side of the room and men on the other side of the room.

4. Questions will be posed one at a time and alternating between groups. For instance, the first question might be posed to the women. The second then going to the men.

5. These are the ground rules for the discussion:
This is a sensitive and scary topic. You may have had a lot of previous experience with sex or no experience at all. Either way is OK. From a strictly statistical standpoint—some of you have experienced intercourse, some of you are virgins, some of you are gay, lesbian, or bisexual.
You need to respect each others' beliefs and values, even if they are different from your own.
You need to really listen to each other–derogatory

comments or statements about others will not be tolerated.

No one will be forced to say anything, but everyone is expected to listen to what is being said.

Only share to the degree you are comfortable.

Speak for yourself. Use "I" statements.

7. Questions are posed until time is over.

Concluding Remarks

Research has shown that you learn a lot from eachother. This is only natural since the amount of time you spend with your peers is much greater then the time you spend in the classroom. Issues related to sexuality are classic examples of the power of this form of "peer education". After you complete this activity, ask yourself the following questions:

a. What did you learn about yourself from this experience?
b. What did you learn about others?

WHAT HAPPENS NEXT?

Purpose To learn more about how men and women are similar and different in their views on sexuality.

Objectives To provide an opportunity for you to learn about gender differences in views of sexuality without fear of embarrassment, to provide a safe environment in which you can discuss important issues relating to sexuality, and to provide an opportunity for you to share their attitudes and beliefs about sexuality with each other.

Supplies Large piece of paper, markers, masking tape.

Time The exercise can range from 30 minutes to over an hour depending on how many questions are raised and how involved the discussion becomes.

Instructions
1. The class is divided with women on one side of the room and men on the other side of the room. It is best, but not necessary, if the two groups cannot hear each other discuss things.

2. Each group receives a couple large sheets of paper and markers.

3. You are now going to explore the issue of human sexuality. This is a complicated, sensitive, scary topic. You may have had a lot of previous experience with sex or no experience at all. Either way is OK. From a strictly statistical standpoint—some of you have experienced intercourse and some of you are virgins. Some of you are heterosexual and some of you are gay, lesbian, or bisexual. You should try not to make any assumptions about each other or judge each other in any way by what is said.

4. These are the ground rules for the discussion:
You need to respect each others' beliefs and values, even if they are different from your own;
You need to really listen to each other–derogatory comments or statements about others will not be tolerated;
No one will be forced to say or do anything but everyone is expected to listen to what is being said;
You should only share to the degree you are comfortable;
Speak for yourself. Use "I" statements.

5. At the bottom of one sheet of newsprint, write the words "First Meet". At the top of the same sheet, write "Have Sex". Now write down all the things that need to happen from the time you "first meet" someone to the time you "have sex" with them." Order is not important at this stage of the exercise.

6. Now number the activities in the order in which they should occur and recopy your list in order.

7. Once each group has their prioritized list completed, share what you've written with the other group. Refrain from asking for clarification until the complete list has been shared. When the complete list has been shared, ask if the other group has any questions. Allow the group to respond to these questions. Repeat the sharing for the other group's list.

8. How similar and different are the two lists?

Concluding Remarks

Sexuality is an extremely complicated area of human life. It is important to remember that differences exist both between the genders and also within each gender. How one woman acts will be different from the way another woman acts, even in the same situation. The same is true of men. After you complete this activity, ask yourself the following questions:

a. What did you learn about your own gender from this experience?
b. What did you learn about the other gender?

JOURNAL ENTRY—SEX

Sex can be a very scary subject, especially in this time of AIDS. While a large percentage of high school and college students have engaged in some form of sexual activity, many others have not. The only way to be completely safe from AIDS is abstinence. Write a letter to an imaginary friend who is still in high school and is deciding whether or not to have sex for the first time. Advise your friend about what you believe he or she should do and outline reasons for the advice you've given.

Resources

Bach, R. (1984). The Bridge Across Forever. New York: Dell.

Bloomfield, H., Vettese, S., and Kory, R. (1989). Lifemates. New York: Signet.

Burns, D. (1985). Intimate Connections. New York: Signet.

Colgrove, M., Bloomfield, H., & McWilliams, P. (1976). How to Survive the Loss of a Love. New York: Bantam.

Farrell, W. (1974). The Liberated Man. New York: Random House.

Farrell, W. (1986). Why Men Are the Way They Are. New York: Berkley.

Fisher, B. (1981). Rebuilding. San Luis Obispo, CA: Impact.

Forward, S. (1991). Obsessive Love. New York: Bantam.

Funk, R. (1993). Stopping Rape. Philadelphia, PA: New Society.

Godek, G. (1991). 1001 Ways to Be Romantic. Boston: Casablanca.

Hendricks, G. and Hendricks, K. (1990). Conscious Loving. New York: Bantam.

Hughes, J. and Sandler, B. (1987). "Friends" Raping Friends—Could It Happen to You? Project on the Status of Women, Association of American Colleges.

Olson, K. (1975). Can You Wait Till Friday? Greenwich, CT: Fawcett.

Parrot, A and Bechhofer, L. (Eds.). (1992). Acquaintance Rape: The Hidden Crime. New York: John Wiley and Sons.

Tannen, D. (1990). You Just Don't Understand. New York: Ballantine.

Warshaw, R. (1988). I Never Called It Rape. New York: Harper & Row.

Student Health Center & Student Counseling Center

Local Planned Parenthood Center

LESSON 20

DATING

There's Nothing to Do

Purpose To determine inexpensive things to do on a date.

Objectives To generate a list of inexpensive things to do on a date then brainstorm with others to create even more activities.

Instructions
1. List ten things you could do on a date that would each cost $10.00 or less.

   1.

   2.

   3.

   4.

   5.

   6.

   7.

   8.

   9.

   10.

2. Get into small groups and share your lists.

3. Now get creative and brainstorm in your groups as many more activities as possible in five minutes. Be sure to write down your ideas.

4. Get someone in each group to type up their list and bring copies to the next class for everyone. Now everyone in the class has a list of literally a hundred things to do that are very inexpensive.

Concluding Remarks

Dating doesn't have to be an expensive activity. When you are first getting to know someone new, it's even more important to do things that let you get to know each other better. By being creative, you'll discover that it's often the cheapest things that turn out to be the most fun. After you complete this activity, ask yourself the following questions:

a. Think about recent times that have been enjoyable or fun for you. What were you doing? Were you spending a lot of money? If yes, could you have had as much fun without spending as much money as you did?

b. How important is spending money when having fun with a friend?

DATING DO'S AND DON'TS

Purpose   Develop a heightened sense of what you and others like and don't like about dating.

Objectives   In a gender-based group, to generate a list of things you like about dating and things you don't like and then use these lists to stimulate a discussion about dating practices.

Supplies   Two poster-sized pieces of paper per group and markers.

Instructions

1. Divide the class with women on one side of the room and men on the other. Give each group two large pieces of paper and markers. At the top of one piece of paper write "I really like it when my dating partner . . ." and on the top of the other piece of paper write "I really hate it when my dating partner . . ."

2. As a group, brainstorm and write as many things as you can think of on the first piece of paper. Repeat this process on the second sheet of paper.

3. Now present your list to the other group, taking turns so that both "I really like..." lists are presented first followed by both of the "I really hate..." lists.

4. As a large group discuss the following:

Do you need any statements to be clarified or explained?

How were your lists similar?

How were they different?

Can you make any generalizations about what you as a class really like and really hate about the dating experience?

Concluding Remarks Dating can be, and often is, a very scary experience. Because of this, it's also something that students tend to talk about only with close friends. By sharing in a large group, what you and your peers really like and really hate about dating, you'll probably gain some insights into this mysterious activity and how to navigate these treacherous waters. After you complete this activity, ask yourself the following questions:

a. Have you done any of the things in either list when you were out on a date? How did your date react when you did it?
b. Think about your best date. Did any of the things on the "I really like..." list happen? Did any of the things on the "I really hate..." list happen?
c. Think about your worst date. Did any of the things on the "I really like..." list happen? Did any of the things on the "I really hate..." list happen?

Lesson 20 Dating

DATE? WHAT'S A DATE?

Purpose To learn about dating in the 90s.

Objectives Through group discussion, to learn how other students handle the dating ritual—from meeting people, to letting them know you're interested, to actually going on a date.

Instructions 1. In the following table, think of three ideas for each of the following questions. Your answers may come from ways that you have been successful in these situations, or ways that you think will be successful.

How do you meet people?	Where do you go to meet people?
1.	1.
2.	2.
3.	3.

How do you let someone know you're interested in them?	What's the best way to let someone know you're not interested in them?
1.	1.
2.	2.
3.	3.

How do you ask someone out?	How do you turn someone down?
1.	1.
2.	2.
3.	3.

2. Pair up with someone else and compare lists. In what ways were your lists similar or different?

Similar:

Different:

3. Now as a class combine all your lists on the board. Are the similarities and differences still true?

Concluding Remarks

Dating can be a very stressful experience. Wondering where and how to meet people, facing the fear of possibly being rejected, wondering how to gently but firmly turn someone down—all of these are real dilemmas for anyone involved in dating situations. Hopefully this exercise has provided you with some ideas of how to handle some of the more stressful of dating situations. After you complete this activity, ask yourself the following questions:

a. What parts of the discussion did you find most useful?
b. Think back on a situation where you broke up with someone or someone broke up with you. Based on the ideas generated above, would you have handled the situation differently?

JOURNAL ENTRY—DATING

Think about a person you'd be interested in dating. This person may be real or imaginary. Make a journal entry describing this person. Why are you interested in this person? What qualities does this person possess that makes him or her so attractive to you?

RESOURCES

Bach, R. (1984). <u>The Bridge Across Forever</u>. New York: Dell.

Bloomfield, H., Vettese, S., and Kory, R. (1989). <u>Lifemates</u>. New York: Signet.

Burns, D. (1985). <u>Intimate Connections</u>. New York: Signet.

Coleman, E. and Edwards, B. (1979). <u>Brief Encounters</u>. Garden City, NY: Anchor.

Colgrove, M., Bloomfield, H., & McWilliams, P. (1976). <u>How to Survive the Loss of a Love</u>. New York: Bantam.

Covey, S. (1989). <u>The 7 Habits of Highly Effective People</u>. New York: Simon & Schuster.

Farrell, W. (1974). <u>The Liberated Man</u>. New York: Random House.

Farrell, W. (1986). <u>Why Men Are the Way They Are</u>. New York: Berkley.

Fisher, B. (1981). <u>Rebuilding</u>. San Luis Obispo, CA: Impact.

Forward, S. (1991). <u>Obsessive Love</u>. New York: Bantam.

Funk, R. (1993). <u>Stopping Rape</u>. Philadelphia, PA: New Society.

Godek, G. (1991). <u>1001 Ways to Be Romantic</u>. Boston: Casablanca.

Hughes, J. and Sandler, B. (1987). <u>"Friends" Raping Friends—Could It Happen to You?</u> Project on the Status of Women, Association of American Colleges.

Olson, K. (1975). <u>Can You Wait Till Friday?</u> Greenwich, CT: Fawcett.

Parrot, A and Bechhofer, L. (Eds.). (1992). <u>Acquaintance Rape: The Hidden Crime</u>. New York: John Wiley and Sons.

Powell, J. (1990). <u>Why Am I Afraid to Tell You Who I Am?</u> Allen, TX: Tabor.

Powell, J. (1982). <u>Why Am I Afraid to Love?</u> Allen, TX: Tabor.

Powell, J. (1985). <u>Will the Real Me Please Stand Up?</u> Allen, TX: Tabor. (Communication focus)

Tannen, D. (1990). <u>You Just Don't Understand</u>. New York: Ballantine.

Warshaw, R. (1988). <u>I Never Called It Rape</u>. New York: Harper & Row.

LESSON 21

WELLNESS

Workout to Wellness

Purpose   To engage in physical activity designed to feel invigorated.

Objective   In a group setting, to learn methods for feeling invigorated and interacting with others.

Supplies   A source of uplifting music and a carpeted or matted room. (An aerobics room would be ideal.) All participants should dress in comfortable, loose-fitting exercise clothes, including socks, but no shoes.

Instructions

1. The entire class should get in a circle with their shoulders touching. Turn so that you are facing the back of the person on your right. Now give that person a back rub. Everyone in the circle is getting a back rub at the same time. Give feedback such as rub lower or higher, rub harder or smoother, etc. The back rub should last for at least five minutes. Learn to wallow in the enjoyment!

2. Move into the circle and closer to the person in front of you. Simultaneously, slowly bend your knees and sit on the lap of the person behind you. Be careful; don't hurt the person you are sitting on. Everyone should be able to sit down in relative comfort.

3. Slowly stand up and form two parallel lines facing each other. Sit down on the rug or mat with you feet out in front of you lightly touching the feet of the person across from you. Lightly rub the bottoms of the feet of the person in front of you with your toes, soles, and heels. This foot rub should last for at least five minutes.

4. Stand up and extend your hands out in front of you touching the palms of the person across from you. As if you hands were resting on a mirror, move your hands up and down and side to side. Go down to the floor and up as high as you can without loosing contact with your partner's palms. This palm mirroring should last for at least five minutes.

5. Regroup so that there are six or seven people in each group. Take turns doing trust falls. Have one member turn his or her back to the other members of the group. Close your eyes and cross your arms over your chest and slowly fall backward. The other members of the group should catch the person who is

Lesson 21 Wellness   **151**

falling. Ultimately, the falling person should be gently placed on the floor by the other members of the group. Each group member should do one to three trust falls.

6. The final part of this exercise is to regroup in a circle. Give the person on your right a back rub. Turn and give one to the person on your left.

Concluding Remarks

You've just had a physical workout while experiencing the soothing power of the human touch. You have learned to rely on your group members during the trust fall. The foot rub and palm mirror exercises are a form of adult play which is a lost art in modern society. After you complete this activity, ask yourself the following questions:

a. How did it feel to be touched?
b. How did it feel to do the touching?
c. How did your body feel after this exercise?

ESTABLISHING A WELLNESS PLAN

Purpose To establish a total wellness plan for yourself.

Objective In a group setting, to define wellness in terms of exercise, nourishment and rest in the three components of your life: mind, body and spirit.

Time The exercise should take 45-60 minutes depending on the size of the group.

Instructions

1. Divide the class into three groups based on their interest in exercise, nourishment, and rest. The groups should be approximately the same size.

2. Each group should elect a chairperson or leader to keep them focused on their task. The leader should keep good notes so that he or she can make a report back to the other two groups at the end of the exercise.

3. Each member of the group should take a few minutes to outline what wellness means to them in their area, i.e. exercise, nourishment, and rest. They should consider wellness in the three dimensions of mind, body, and spirit.

4. After each group member has taken a few minutes to outline their thoughts, the group should conduct a consensus task to establish the key elements of wellness in their area. Combine each members thoughts into one list on a sheet of paper.

5. After all the definitions of wellness have been combined into one list, the leader should conduct a group consensus task to rank-order all the elements of wellness. The group needs to decide which is the most important element, the second most important element, and so on. Each group must arrive at this list without averaging, "horse trading" (I'll support yours if you support mine), or taking a majority vote. This ranking should result as a result of discussion and consensus until every group member feels comfortable with the ranking.

6. Once each group has completed this task, the leader of each group should present a report on the results of their consensus on the three areas of wellness.

Concluding Remarks

Students define wellness in many ways. Will Keim believes there must be a dynamic balance between exercise, nourishment and rest. Wellness is like a three-legged stool. Without each leg of wellness, the stool will topple and fall. It is your task to find this balance and demonstrate it in your mind, body and spirit. After you complete this activity, ask yourself the following questions:

a. What does wellness mean to you?
b. Do you have a well-balanced program of wellness in the three areas of exercise, nourishment, and rest?
c. Does your program address the areas of your mind, body and spirit in equal amounts? What areas are getting short-changed?
d. What is your action plan to improve your wellness?

JOURNAL ACTIVITY ON WELLNESS

With all the emphasis in the last twenty years on fitness and the more recent "wellness" movement, it is surprising to see the increase in smoking, drinking, and eating disorders on college campuses. Basically, your body is a temple. It is the vessel which carries you through your journey of life. A weak, ineffective vessel will deprive you of a long and fruitful life. What does wellness mean to you? Have you neglected any component(s) of wellness: exercise, nourishment, or rest? Have you neglected any element(s): mind, body, or spirit? What is your action plan for improving your wellness? What have you learned about the strengths and weaknesses of your wellness plan?

RESOURCES

Bailey, C. (1978). <u>The New Fit or Fat</u>. Boston: Houghton Mifflin Company.

LESSON 22

ETHICS

WHAT I MEAN WHEN I SAY ETHICS

Purpose   To define your ethical standards.

Objective   To answer questions on your ethical standards and show how you have implemented those standards in your life, then to understand another person's ethical experiences and decisions.

Instructions   1.   Select a partner you can trust. It may be a classmate, a friend, or your roommate.

2.   Your partner should begin the conversation by asking you the following series of questions:

a.   What does it mean to you to be an ethical person?

b.   What are the qualities of an ethical person?

c.   To what degree do you possess these ethical qualities?

d.   How have you incorporated these qualities in your decision-making process?

e. How can you learn more effective ethical decision-making skills in your life?

3. Don't answer these questions with brief answers. Give your partner specific examples in your personal experience which show these qualities. Describe ethical dilemmas in your own life and how you handled them. Also, provide examples of how your mentors or people you admire have handled similar issues.

4. Now reverse the process and ask your partner the questions listed above. Use this experience as a learning opportunity to expand your awareness of another person's ethical issues and dilemmas.

Concluding Remarks

Everyone is confronted with ethical issues in their lives. Mature ethical decision-making is based on your own ethical standards in the context of a larger matrix of rules of fairness and honesty. This exercise will help you clarify your ethics. After you complete this activity, ask yourself the following questions:

a. What have you learned about your ethical standards?
b. Do your standards vary with the situation or are they unchanging?
c. Do you have the same standards for your friends and enemies?
d. By what rules or concepts do you arrive at ethical decisions?
e. How do your ethical standards differ from others?

CASE STUDIES IN ETHICS

Purpose To explore ethical decision-making.

Objective To explore three case studies and the ethical decisions necessary to deal with the problems presented.

Instructions
1. What is your first reaction to a decision-making situation: thinking, feeling or acting? Think about decisions you have had to make recently and be very honest with yourself. Break into three groups based on which of the three activities you do first in decision-making:

Think   Feel   Act

2. Elect a chair and recorder for each group. The chair is responsible for keeping the discussion focused and making sure every group member participates in the discussion. The recorder is responsible for documenting the decision-making process and the ultimate decision of the group.

3. The "think" groups' case study is:

Three roommates are all involved in the college radio station. Two are on the Executive Board and the other is a deejay. A major problem this year has been a large number of missing compact discs (CDs). Who could have taken them? Only Executive Board members have keys to the radio station. Late night disc jockeys are the prime suspects.

One Saturday, the deejay is trying to locate his new shoes and looks in a box under his roommate's bed. In that box he/she finds over 25 CDs with the radio station's identifying sticker on them. What should the roommate do?

   a. Confront the roommate
   b. Turn the roommate in to the Executive Board
   c. Tell the Director of Student Activities
   d. None of the above
   e. All of the above
   f. Something else

In a group setting, decide on what to do, the important ethical issues and the ultimate ramifications of your decision.

4. The "feel" group's case study is:

Two best friends are Chair and Vice-Chair of the programming board on campus. During the beginning of the year, they work harmoniously together. However, as the year progresses, the Vice-Chair begins to slack off due to a heavy load of classes. The duties of the Vice-Chair are not getting done, so the Chair picks up the slack and covers for the best friend. The Vice-Chair comes to some meetings late and misses some altogether. The advisor and other members start to notice the problem. The Chair's grades start to suffer because she is doing two jobs. What should the Chair do?

a. Confront the Vice-Chair
b. Impeach the Vice-Chair
c. Tell the advisor
d. None of the above
e. All of the above
f. Something else

In a group setting, decide on what to do, the important ethical issues and the ultimate ramifications of your decision.

5. The "act" group's case study is:

A group of students is helping a biology professor with some research. To help them do their work, the professor has given each of them a key to the lab room so they can work at night. Normally, only professors have the key to the lab. One student surreptitiously makes duplicates of the lab key and sells it to his friends for $10. Rumors begin to circulate concerning the availability of lab keys for cash. The department chair goes to the lab one night and finds one of the student researchers there with four other students and three lab keys on the table. What should the department chair do?

a. Confront the student researcher
b. Kick them all out and confiscate the keys
c. Bring the student researcher to the Judicial Board
d. None of the above
e. All of the above
f. Something else

In a group setting, decide on what to do, the important ethical issues and the ultimate ramifications of your decision.

6. Get back together in one large group and have each recorder present the group's decision and decision-making process. How does the process and ultimate decisions differ between groups?

Concluding Remarks

Everyone is faced with ethical dilemmas almost every day. Some may not be as serious as the cases here, others may be even more serious. To know your values and to know how you might react to these situations is important to making an ethical decision when you are faced with a real situation. After you complete this activity, ask yourself the following questions:

a. How do your values affect your ethical decision-making?
b. How do your friendships affect your ethics?
c. Are your ethical standards independent of other issues?
d. How does your personality type affect your decisions (i.e. thinkers - analytical; feelers - emotional; actors - rational)?
e. What have you learned about your character and integrity in these case studies?

JOURNAL ACTIVITY ON ETHICS

Make a list of people you admire most. They can be living or dead; fictitious or real; someone you know or someone you do not know; from the present or from history. List several ethical qualities you find particularly attractive in these people. Do you have these qualities? What things can you do to develop these qualities in yourself?

LESSON 23

HATE

Hate—It's All Around You

Purpose   Discover people or events that demonstrate how prevalent hate is in the world and think of ways to combat that hate.

Objectives   To identify examples of hate that are evident in the newspaper every day and to brainstorm in a group possible ways that individuals or groups can combat these feelings of hate.

Supplies   Daily newspaper

Instructions   1. Identify a newspaper that you can read or skim on a daily basis. You may not want to use your school paper because it may not have much international, national or local news in it.

     2. Read or skim the paper for a week. Identify as many articles as you can that describe some form of hate or hateful acts that one person or persons has done to another. Clip or copy these articles if possible. Take some notes about the articles including who did what to whom, why they did it, etc. Also note any articles that propose ways to end hate.

Article Title:

Publication:

Date of Publication:

What happened?

Why did it happen?

Other comments

Lesson 23   Hate

Article Title:
Publication:
Date of Publication:
What happened?

Why did it happen?

Other comments

Article Title:
Publication:
Date of Publication:
What happened?

Why did it happen?

Other comments

Article Title:
Publication:
Date of Publication:
What happened?

Why did it happen?

Other comments

Article Title:
Publication:
Date of Publication:
What happened?

Why did it happen?

Other comments

3. In class, talk about the articles that you found. Did hate seem prevalent or rare? Did you notice any consistencies among these acts? Did you find any articles that proposed ways to try to end hate?

Concluding Remarks

Examples of hate are all around us. They occur every day, in every town and city, in every state and nation. Whether it takes the form of hateful, spiteful words or physical abuse of another person, hate destroys everyone and everything it touches. Hopefully, this exercise showed you how prevalent hate is and moved you to think about ways to diminish it in our society. After you complete this activity, ask yourself the following questions:

a. How close is hate or hateful acts to your life?
b. In what ways can you eliminate hate or at least lessen its pervasiveness in your life?
c. In what ways can you or groups that you belong to lessen the pervasiveness of hate in your community?

HATE ON SCREEN

Purpose To observe how hate is portrayed in selected movies and the effect of that portrayal on your life and in your community.

Objectives To watch a film that focuses on hate and experience the emotions of that film, then discuss how people in the movie acted upon their feelings of hate and discover the consequences of hate for all of the people involved.

Supplies Video of a film which has hate as a major theme. Examples would include "Schindler's List", "Mississippi Burning", or "Philadelphia".

Time Three hours to watch the movie. Could take over an hour for class discussion.

Instructions Watch a movie that focuses on hate. This can be done alone, in small groups, or as a whole class. This may be a powerful, emotional experience for many of you. Discuss the film by answering the following questions:

Who hated whom in the film? Why did they hate them?

What actions or behaviors resulted from these feelings of hate? How did the person or person who were the objects of the hate respond?

Lesson 23 Hate

What effect did hate have upon those who did the hating?

What thoughts and feelings did you have as you watched the film?

What did you learn about hate from watching this movie?

How can you apply what you learned to your daily lives?

Concluding Remarks

Hate is obviously a very powerful emotion, as evidenced in the movie that you watched and discussed. Hating another individual or members of a group for any reason does horrible things to everyone involved. After you complete this activity, ask yourself the following questions:

a. In the film you watched, those who hated so viciously were viewed as "normal" members of their society. How could this happen?
b. How can supposedly "good" people hate other people?
c. How does this hatred that is accepted by a society affect the society? How can these effects be mitigated?

JOURNAL ENTRY ON HATE

Hate is an extremely powerful emotion. So powerful, in fact, that we often deny its very existence inside of us. Yet each of us has been filled with hate or rage at some time in our life. Try to remember the last time you hated someone or something. Who or what was the object of your rage? When and under what circumstances did it first appear? How and why did it grow in magnitude? What effect did it have upon the object of your rage? What did you do about it?

RESOURCES

Bellah, R., et. al. (1987). <u>Habits of the Heart</u>. New York: Harper and Row.

Buber, M. (1958). <u>I and Thou</u>. New York: Charles Scribner's Sons.

Evans, N & Wall, V. (Eds.) (1989). <u>Beyond Tolerance: Gays, Lesbians, and Bisexuals on Campus</u>. Alexandria, VA: American College Personnel Association.

Ford, C. (1994). <u>We Can All Get Along</u>. New York: Dell.

Frankl, V. (1984). <u>Man's Search for Meaning</u>. New York: Simon and Schuster.

Giovanni, N. (1992). <u>Racism 101</u>. New York: Morrow.

Isaacson, J. (1991). <u>Seed of Sarah</u>. Urbana, IL: University of Illinois.

Levi, P. (1960). <u>Survival in Auschwitz</u>. New York: Macmillan.

Niedergang, M. (1994). <u>Can't We All Just Get Along? A Race Manual for Discussion Programs on Racism and Race Relations</u>. Pomfret, CT: Study Circles Resource Center.

Peck, M. (1987). <u>The Different Drum</u>. New York: Simon and Schuster.

Peck, M. (1992). <u>A World Waiting to Be Born</u>. New York: Bantam.

Whitmyer, C. (Ed.). (1993). <u>In the Company of Others</u>. New York: Tarcher/Perigee.

LESSON 24

SPIRITUALITY

LET THE SPIRIT BE WITH YOU

Purpose To get in touch with your spirituality.

Objective With others, to explore the meaning of spirituality and determine what effect it has on your life.

Instructions
1. Pair up with a person you can trust. A member of your class would be best, but a friend or your roommate would be fine.

2. Answer the following questions. Try to give answers longer than one phrase or sentence. Provide specific examples to clarify your answers for each question. Your partner should note ideas that especially move, inspire, or trouble him or her.

   a. What is your definition of a higher power?
   b. How does the spirit give you hope?
   c. How does the spirit bring out the best in you?
   d. How does the spirit help you be tolerant of others?
   e. How does the spirit contribute to your education?
   f. How does the spirit teach you love?
   g. How does your vision of spirituality effect your behavior?
   h. How does spirituality manifest itself in your life?

3. Now have your partner can answer these questions. Note ideas that are especially moving, inspiring, or troubling to you.

4. Share and discuss each of your reactions. For example, " I liked it when you compared God to the tides; sometimes it's in and sometimes it's out, but you know it will always return." This should be done in a spirit of openness, nonjudgmentally. Try to understand your partner's reaction, however you do not have to agree with it.

Concluding Remarks It has become unfashionable to discuss "your deeper self; the spirit within." However, several commentators, such as Scott Peck, have identified the lack of spirituality in our lives as the major cause of the erosion of community spirit today. After you complete this activity, ask yourself the following questions:

   a. What have you learned about your own spirituality?
   b. What purpose does the spirit serve in your life?
   c. How does your spirituality make you a better person?
   d. How can you learn to better understand and accept other's spirituality?

DISCUSSION ON SPIRITUALITY

Purpose To define spirituality and establish how it can manifest itself in your life.

Objective In a group setting, to define spirituality and how it reveals itself in your life.

Time This exercise should take 45 to 60 minutes depending on the depth of the discussions.

Instructions

1. Divide the class into groups of eight to ten students. Each group should elect a leader and a recorder for the group. The leader will make certain the group process moves along smoothly and that all members of the group are participating. The recorder will take notes and summarize the group's results of the brainstorming session for the other groups.

2. Each member of the group should individually take a few minutes to reflect on the following two questions:

What does spirituality mean to you?

How has the "spirit," as you define it, been a part of your life?

3. After each group member has taken a few minutes to reflect on these questions, the leader should have each person write down their definition of spirituality in a list where every group member can see it.

4. Once each member has written down their definition, the leader should facilitate a group discussion on spirituality and its unique meaning to each individual.

5. Then, each member of the group should go back to their paper and write down one example of how the "spirit" has been a part of their life.

6. Once again, the leader should facilitate a group discussion on the manifestation of the "spirit" in their lives both large and small.

7. Once each group has completed these tasks, the recorder of each group should present a report on the results of their group discussions to the entire class.

Concluding Remarks

It's amazing how diverse and rich individual experience of spirituality really is! Some individuals experience it on a daily basis, while others see it very infrequently, or not at all. After you complete this activity, ask yourself the following questions:

a. What does spirituality mean to me?
b. Did discussions with fellow students enrich and broaden my concept of the spirit's manifestation in my life?
c. What new things have I learned about spirituality from this exercise?

Journal Activity on Spirituality

People sometimes think that spirituality can only manifest itself in grandiose terms. A cancer patient miraculously recovers; a passenger misses a plane and it crashes. Spirituality can also be as profound in little things. The first robin of spring; the first crocus; the brilliant leaves of a New England fall; the sound of surf breaking on the shore; the chance meeting of an old friend. Spirituality can manifest itself in wonders large and small. The key is to learn to recognize it and appreciate it whenever it happens. Do you notice the small and large miracles in life? Do you count on these miracles (like when a check arrives just when you run out of money) or do you plan ahead and if they happen, all the better? Write you answers to these questions as a stream of consciousness, free flowing and uninhibited, then read back over what you have written.

RESOURCES

Peck, M. S., MD. (1978). <u>The Road Less Traveled</u>. New York: Simon and Schuster.

Williams, M. (1983). <u>The Velveteen Rabbit or How Toys Become Real</u>. New York: Henry Holt and Company.

LESSON 25

SENIORS

"I" Messages

Purpose To provide you with positive statements about yourself and your abilities as you prepare to "start over."

Objective To create a list of "I" messages about your abilities and then reinforce these messages by saying them aloud to yourself so you will internalize them and get confidence about your ability to start over and be successful in new situations.

Instructions "I" messages are short statements that reinforce positive attitudes and abilities of which you are proud. Create a list of positive "I" messages about yourself and your abilities that builds/promotes your self-esteem which you can review whenever you find yourself in a new situation and needing a boost. These "I" messages might include statements such as "I love a challenge" or "I'm going to do a fine job" or "I am very capable of handling a new situation."

Concluding Remarks

You now have a list of positive statements that will reinforce you and your abilities. By posting these statements in a visible place, you can review them, by both reading them to yourself and saying them aloud, whenever you find yourself in a new situation and feeling like a 'freshman.' After you complete this activity, ask yourself the following questions:

a. How did you feel as you wrote down positive "I" messages about yourself? How did you feel as you said positive "I" messages about yourself?
b. Will hearing be believing for you in regards to these "I" messages? Why or why not?
c. What did you learn about yourself from this activity?
d. How can you apply this activity to other aspects of your life?

LOVE OF LEARNING ESSAY

Purpose To identify what the love of learning is to you and how you will incorporate your love of learning in the new situations you will face after you leave college.

Objective You will face many new learning opportunities when you leave college that will require you to learn new information. These new beginnings may be challenging for you but if you understand why you love to learn, you will face these new beginnings as opportunities rather than obstacles.

Instructions 1. Write a short essay on what the love of learning means to you.

To me, love of learning means...

2. Review your essay and identify ways you will apply your responses to the new learning opportunities you will encounter after graduation:

Concluding Remarks

By translating a love of learning philosophy into situations, abilities, skills, etc., you will have a better understanding of how 'transferable' your ability is to be a continual learner. Recognizing this will allow you to face new challenges as opportunities to expand your learning rather than as obstacles to challenge your learning. After you complete this activity, ask yourself the following questions:

a. Were you surprised by any of your responses in identifying what a love of learning meant to you? If so, what surprised you?
b. In reading your essay, what strikes you most about your responses?
c. What does your essay tell you about yourself?
d. Did you realize/learn anything new about yourself from this activity?
e. How will understanding what a love of learning personally means to you be beneficial in your future learning situations?

JOURNAL ENTRY ON SENIORS

Describe the thoughts and feelings you have about "starting over" and being the new kid on the block once again.

RESOURCES

Bridges, W. (1980). <u>Transitions: Making Sense of Life's Changes</u>. Reading, MA: Addison-Wesley Publishing Company.

Bridges, W. (1993). <u>Managing Transitions: Making the Most of Change</u>. Reading, MA: Addison-Wesley Publishing Company.

Schlossberg, N. (1989). <u>Overwhelmed: Coping with Life's Ups and Downs</u>. Lexington, MA: D.C. Heath.

LESSON 26

HOMECOMING

TOTO...THERE'S NO PLACE LIKE HOME

Purpose   To determine the benefits and potential problems of moving home after graduation.

Objective   To examine the potential positive and negative results of moving home after graduation.

Time   This exercise should take 45-60 minutes depending on the depth of your discussion.

Instructions   1. Pair up with a person you can trust. A member of your class would be best, but a friend or your roommate would be fine.

2. Tell your partner ten responses for each of the following two sentences:

It would be great to move home after graduation because...

It would be a problem to move home after graduation because...

An example of these sentence completions might be:

I could get to know my younger siblings better.
I could get to know my parents as a more mature, young adult.
I could save money.
I wouldn't have the freedom to come and go as I want.
I can only work in the area, rather than looking for a job anywhere.

3. After you have completed the two sentences ten times each, switch roles with your partner and have him/her complete the two sentences. Your partner may have the same answers or different answers, depending on his or her particular situation and feelings.

4. Once you have completed this exercise, have a brief discussion with your partner weighing the pros and cons of moving home after graduation.

Concluding Remarks   Obviously, there are positive and negative reasons for moving home after graduation. However sometimes it is not a decision of your choice but rather a necessity. It is critical to realistically evaluate this decision and, to the extent possible, prepare for it.

After you complete this activity, ask yourself the following questions:

a. Are you optimistic or pessimistic about a potential move home?
b. What will be the major positive and negative issues you will need to deal with?
c. How can you prepare your family and yourself for the move home after graduation?

CASE STUDIES

Purpose   To explore the potential implications of a decision to move back home after graduation.

Objective   To explore three case studies of potential situations which might arise if you were to move back home after graduation and to brainstorm effective ways to resolve them.

Instructions 1. Divide the class into three equal groups. Each group must elect a leader and a recorder for the group. The leader will keep the group on track and make sure everyone participates. The recorder will take good notes to make a presentation to the other two groups on its solution to the problem presented in the case study.

The first group's case study is:

You are approaching graduation day and you do not have a job yet. Your father has been badgering you to come home and start to take over the lucrative family business. You have no alternative but to move home, but you have no interest in the family business and want to purse a social service career. You need to have a discussion with your father about these issues. How should you handle it?

In a group, decide on what to say, what points your father will bring up such as "just work part-time in the business until something else shows up so you can have spending money," and how to deal with all his points.

The second group's case study is:

You have been living at home for three months and things have been going very well. On a Saturday night, some old college friends call and say they are in town for a couple of days attending a conference. They invite you down to their hotel room for a party. You stay out until 5:00 am. When you arrive home, your mother is sitting up in the living room with tears running down her cheeks. She states, "I thought you had been killed in a car accident. Why didn't you call to say you would be home so late?"

In a group, decide on what to say to your mother and determine what counterpoints she will bring up and how to respond to them.

The third group's case study is:

You have been living at home for eight months and you finally have landed a great job three hundred miles away from home. Your former roommate already works in that town and needs a roommate. At dinner that night you announce your job and your plans to move out as soon as possible. You have enjoyed your eight months stay at home and it was much better than you had anticipated. You have noticed how much your parents have changed (or was it you who did the changing?) and want to express your appreciation. What should you say and how should you respond to their sadness that you are leaving?

In a group, decide on what you should say to them and how you would respond to any issues they may bring up. How can you express your true gratitude to them?

---

2. Get back together in one large group and have each group recorder summarize the case study and the group's decisions on how to handle the situation.

Concluding Remarks

Transitions can be difficult times for everyone. In the past a college education was a guaranteed "meal ticket" to a good job and a career of your choice. The lengthy recession which hit white-collar workers hard and increased world competition has had a detrimental effect on college students' job prospects. New flexible responses are necessary on the parts of students and parents alike. After you complete this activity, ask yourself the following questions:

a. Could you move back home if you felt you had to?
b. What impediments would there be to a harmonious stay back home?
c. How would it make you feel about yourself? (i.e. a failure, etc.)
d. What parts of your relationship with your parents need work?

Journal Activity on Homecoming

More and more college graduates are choosing or forced to move home as a transitional stage between college and career. It is important to prepare for this possibility. How do you believe your parents would react to your moving home after graduation? How would you feel about moving home after graduation? How can a "homecoming" provide an opportunity to build a new relationship with your parents based on equality and maturity?

Lesson 27

CONTRIBUTORSHIP

MAKING MY CONTRIBUTION

Purpose To identify how you can set an example and be a contributor toward the individuals and groups with whom you interact on a daily basis.

Objective To come up with ways that you can become a major contributor to groups, such as your friends, your living group companions, the other students at your institution and your local community, on a daily basis by setting an example in small and large ways.

Instructions Making a contribution means setting the example for others. Describe how can you make a contribution to the following groups:

a. My Friends:

b. My Living Group:

c. My Campus/Institution:

d. My Local Community:

Concluding Remarks

Often, we fail to recognize that our words and actions do have an impact on the people who are closest to us--those we interact with on a regular, daily basis. By being aware of the influence you have, you can begin to be a daily contributor to these individuals and groups by setting an example. After you complete this activity, ask yourself the following questions:

a. Have you ever previously thought of yourself as a contributor to your friends, living group, college or local community? Is this a comfortable role in which to see yourself? Why or why not?

b. How do you think people's words and actions might be different if everyone thought of themselves as contributors?

c. Are you aware of an experience where you have set the example for your friends or another group? What was that experience like for you?

CONTRIBUTORS ARE...

Purpose   To acknowledge a significant person in your life whose contributorship has influenced you.

Objective   To reflect on the characteristics of a contributor and identify the person or people in your life who have role-modeled these traits for you. By associating the title contributor with these important people in your life, being a contributor takes on special meaning. Hopefully, by emulating others whom you admire as contributors, you will also become a contributor whose behavior becomes a role model for others.

Instructions   Will Keim (1993) defines contributors as "men and women of character who are open to the ideas of others. They search for better ways to do things, "never say never," and are teachable people who are willing to learn. Contributors are responsible and imaginative and work for the betterment of all concerned" (page 69).

When you read this description, what one person in your life do you think best fits this definition of a contributor? Describe this person below and share how this person has influenced your life.

Concluding Remarks   We imitate the behavior of people we admire. If we admire people who exhibit traits such as openness to ideas, being teachable, responsible, imaginative and never saying never, we admire contributors. The next step is to make these admirable qualities part of who you are--to become an active contributor yourself. After you complete this activity, ask yourself the following questions:

a. How do you feel about the person you identified above as the special contributor in your life? Were you aware of how much this person influenced your life prior to this activity?

b. Is your contributor someone you would describe as a role-model? Which of your contributor's behaviors do you most admire and want to emulate yourself? Why?

Journal Entry on Contributorship

What does leadership by example mean to you? How can you incorporate leadership by example into your daily life?

RESOURCES

Block, P. (1993). <u>Stewardship: Choosing Service Over Self-Interest</u>. New York: Berkley Publishing Group.

Covey, S. R. (1991). <u>Principle-Centered Leadership</u>. New York: Simon & Schuster, Inc.

DePree, M. (1989). <u>Leadership is an Art</u>. New York: Dell Trade.

Editors of Conari Press. (1993). <u>Random Acts of Kindness</u>. Berkeley, CA: Conari Press.

Kelley, R. (1992). <u>The Power of Followership: How to Create Leaders People Want to Follow...and Followers Who Lead Themselves</u>. New York: Doubleday.

Kouzes, J.M. & Posner, B.Z. (1987). <u>The Leadership Challenge: How to Get Extraordinary Things Done in Organizations</u>. San Francisco: Jossey-Bass.

LESSON 28

SUCCESS

THE MEANING OF SUCCESS

Purpose To discover how others have defined what is meant by the concept of "success."

Objectives To research what has been written about success and to gather quotes from others on their definition of success. These definitions will be shared and made into your own personal success poster to use for inspiring yourself on a daily basis.

Supplies A couple sheets of paper and either markers or computer with variable fonts.

Instructions

1. Consider the concept of "success." Go to your library and find at least five different definitions of success and at least five quotes or sayings describing the concept of success.

2. Pick your favorite one or two definitions or quotes. Write the quotes or definitions on separate sheets of paper so that they are large enough to act as a small poster. They could be either hand printed or done on a computer with a large font.

3. Bring your definitions or quotes to class to share with your classmates. Explain how and where you found these particular definitions and why you chose them.

4. Take your "posters" home with you and put them up so you can see them every day and be inspired.

Concluding Remarks

People throughout history have written about success from a variety of different perspectives. These writings from the past can be used to encourage us in the present. The benefit of a daily dose of inspirational writing can be a great antidote for whatever ails you—especially if the malady is a lack of motivation. College can be a challenging time. Be sure to surround yourself with pictures, words, things, and people that inspire you and help encourage the formation of a positive attitude. After you complete this activity ask yourself the following questions:

a. How do you define success?
b. Were there some definitions or quotes about success that did not fit your definition? Why did they not fit?

MY PROUDEST MOMENTS

Purpose To identify and celebrate past accomplishments.

Objectives To identify some of the great successes you've experienced in your life and to use these successes as the basis for an activity designed to help you get to know your classmates better.

Instructions
1. Think of four successes you've experienced in your life They could be small successes, like staying on a diet for one day or remembering to do something you always forget, or big successes, like achieving the grade you wanted in a class or handling a personal situation well.

2. Get into groups of four or five persons.

3. In a few minutes you will be asked to briefly state these four successes and a fifth successful experience which will be a lie. Don't tell your group which experiences are true and which are the fabrications.

4. Go around your group and have each person relate his or her five successes (four true and one lie). When the person is done, other group members must try to figure out which one was the lie. This activity is a great ice breaker and helps you get to know each other a little better.

Concluding Remarks While being successful means different things to different people, we have all had times in our lives when we've been successful at something—sometimes it's something big, sometimes something small. The size of the success is not as important as the being aware of the conditions that contributed to the success and taking pride in your accomplishments. Being positive about ourselves and proud of what we've accomplished in life is an attractive quality to have and can help lead to other successes. Being successful has been called the intersection of preparation and opportunity. After you complete this activity, ask yourself the following questions;

a. How did thinking about your past successes make you feel?
b. What are you doing to prepare yourself for the moment when your next opportunity will appear?

JOURNAL ENTRY—SUCCESS

Is success an internally or externally defined concept for you? Is success defined <u>for you</u> by someone else or do you define it <u>for yourself</u>? What are the benefits and potential drawbacks to your way of defining success?

RESOURCES

Brooks, S. (1990). <u>The Art of Good Living</u>. Boston: Houghton Mifflin.

Covey, S. (1989). <u>The 7 Habits of Highly Effective People</u>. New York: Simon and Schuster.

Cxikszentmiahalyi, M. (1990) <u>Flow</u>. New York: Harper & Row.

John-Roger & McWilliams, P. (1990). <u>Do It!</u> Los Angeles: Prelude.

Myers, D. (1992). <u>The Pursuit of Happiness</u>. New York: Avon.

Tracy, D. (1990). <u>10 Steps to Empowerment</u>. New York: William Morrow.

LESSON 29

WARRIORSHIP

OVERCOMING THE FEAR OF YOURSELF

Purpose   To confront and overcome your fears of yourself.

Objective   To answer partial sentences about your fears and discuss how you can develop your warrior-like qualities to overcome them.

Instructions

1. Select a partner that you feel can be non-judgmental and trusting. This person can be a member of your class, your roommate, or a close friend.

2. Find a quiet place where you will not be disturbed for an hour, where you will have two comfortable lounge chairs. Place the two chairs facing each other and turn on the tape recorder.

3. Your partner will begin by stating a series of partial sentences. Each statement will be read five times; you should complete the statement differently each time. Be as open and honest as you can possibly be. These answers must be given in the strictest confidence. The statements are:

I am afraid when ...
The world scares me when...
I hate it when people ask me to...
I fear myself when...
I can make my world less scary by...
I can overcome my fears by...
If I were not afraid, I would...
If I learned to accept my fears, I would...
As I become a warrior in life, I will...

Your partner should read these statements rapidly repeating each one as quickly as possible. That will help you get in touch with your feelings and avoid shallow, trite responses. A typical series of responses may be:

I am afraid when...people judge me.
I am afraid when...I don't know what is expected of me.
I am afraid when...I feel bullied or intimidated.
I am afraid when...I make people unhappy.
I am afraid when...I fail at an important task.

4. Once you have completed all nine sentences, change tapes and record the answers as you reverse roles with your partner.

You read the partial sentences rapidly as your partner answers them.

5. Once you have completed the exercise, you and your partner should briefly discuss the similarities and differences between your answers. Discuss how each of you can turn these fears into warrior-like qualities. <u>Reaffirm the confidential nature of these replies.</u>

6. Replay the tape periodically with particular emphasis on developing your warrior-like behaviors.

Concluding Remarks

You may be surprised by some of your answers, however many people have these same fears. Overcoming these fears of yourself will require the courage of a warrior. People normally think of Teddy Roosevelt charging up San Juan Hill or Norman Schwarzkopf conquering Saddam Hussein in 100 hours as warriors. But the courage to face your fears day by day and issue by issue requires Herculean effort. You are up to the task. As Susan Jeffers says, "Feel the fear and do it anyway." After you complete this activity, ask yourself the following questions:

a. If you were not fearful, how would you act?
b. How can you become more warrior-like in attacking your fears of yourself?

GROUP ACTIVITY ON WARRIORSHIP

Purpose	To discern the real nature of courage.

Objective	In a group setting, you will clarify your understanding of real courage and establish methods of incorporating warriorship qualities in your personal life.

Instructions	
1. Divide into groups of ten to twelve people.

2. Each group should elect a chairperson and a recorder for the group. The chairperson will make certain everyone participates, while completing the assigned task. The recorder will summarize the results of this exercise for the other groups.

3. Each member of the group should write down examples of people showing real courage in living their lives. An example of some statements would be:

I think people show real courage when they stay with an alcoholic spouse for the good of the children.

I think people show real courage when they conquer their fears (i.e. flying, darkness, heights, etc.)

I think people show real courage when they leave a relationship full of physical and emotional abuse, even when they still love the person.

I think people show real courage when they visit their parent(s) on a regular basis in a nursing home while they are suffering from Alzheimer's disease.

4. After each member of the group suggests ways people show courage, the chairperson should lead a discussion of what the real essence of courage is. This discussion should include how individuals can incorporate warrior-like qualities of courage into their everyday life.

5. Once each group has completed this discussion, the recorder of each group should present a report on the results of their discussion on courage and warriorship.

Concluding Remarks

People show tremendous courage in their everyday life. They are so used to demonstrating courage that they seldom recognize it for what it is. The result of this exercise is to celebrate the courage in your daily life. After you complete this activity, ask yourself the following questions:

a. What is your definition of courage?
b. How do you demonstrate it in your own life?
c. How can you increase your warrior-like behavior in your life?

JOURNAL ACTIVITY ON WARRIORSHIP

What successful accomplishments have you had? Write down five accomplishments in your life. They can be minor or major accomplishments; accomplishments everyone knows about, or private accomplishments. Sometimes success isn't the accomplishment, but trying is. Now write down what you did to help you achieve those accomplishments? Be specific in the things you have done. For example, in order to get elected class president, I put up 1000 posters, I spent two hours on the phone each night campaigning, etc. Review these accomplishments and what you did to overcome your fears. What personality traits did you exhibit in trying to overcome your fears? These are your warrior-like qualities, the qualities that will get you through difficult times. Remember, it's not that you have fears that is important, but how you overcome them.

RESOURCES

Jeffers, S., Ph.D. (1987). <u>Feel the Fear and Do It Anyway</u>. Fawcett Columbine: New York, NY.

LESSON 30

LOVE

LEARNING TO LOVE YOURSELF

Purpose — Learn to love yourself as a person through your thoughts, feelings, and behaviors.

Objective — To identify those thoughts, feelings, and behaviors that are appropriate in a loving relationship and to begin learning to love yourself by applying these thoughts, feelings, and behaviors to yourself.

Instructions — Find a quiet place where you will be uninterrupted for about half an hour and answer the questions below.

If I really loved someone, how would I treat him or her?

If I really loved someone, what thoughts would I have about him or her?

If I really loved someone, what gifts would I give him or her?

Lesson 30 Love

If I really loved someone, how would I act in his or her presence?

If I really loved someone, what would I say or do to let him or her know?

3. Now examine what you wrote. Rephrase the questions by replacing the words "someone" and "him/his" or "her" with "me".

If I really loved me, how would I treat myself?

If I really loved me, what thoughts would I have about myself?

If I really loved me, what gifts would I give myself?

If I really loved me, how would I act?

If I really loved me, how would I remind myself?

4. Compare your answers to the questions in Part 1 to your answers in Part 2. How does the change in the focus of the questions change what you wrote?

5. We often treat others better than we treat ourselves. How can you treat yourself better—in a more loving way?

Concluding Remarks

As Will Keim writes in his book, we must learn to love ourselves before we can really learn to love anyone else. This is often hard to do. This activity should help you to realize how you treat yourself. After you complete this activity, ask yourself the following questions:

a. Have you been treating yourself differently from others? In what ways?
b. Why is it so hard to love ourselves?

THE LOVE MACHINE

Purpose   To recognize the different types of love and to understand the role each plays in life.

Objectives   To determine how different types of love are portrayed on television and how these portrayals might impact you.

Instructions

1. Love has many different definitions and takes many different forms. It can range from agapé love, which is more of a "brotherly" love, to erotic love, which is more "sexual" in nature. Identify at least three different television shows that portray the concept of love in some manner.
2. Watch these shows, writing down how often and in what ways agapé and erotic love are portrayed. (You may want to tape them to show examples in class.)

Show:

Notes:

Show:

Notes:

Lesson 30   Love

Show:

Notes:

---

3. In class, discuss what you noticed. What general patterns did you notice? Was one form of love shown more often than the other? Why do you think this was true? Did you find any other types of love?

Concluding Remarks

The media is a powerful tool in shaping behavior. Of the various kinds of media, television is certainly one of the most powerful. The concept of love is portrayed very differently on soap operas, situation comedies, dramas, talk shows, and music television. After you complete this activity, ask yourself the following questions:

a. How do you think your thoughts and feelings about love have been shaped by television or the movies?
b. How often does agapé love and erotic love play a role in your life? Does one play a larger role than the other?
c. Do any other types of love play a role in your life?

JOURNAL ENTRY ON LOVE

There has undoubtedly been more written about love than any other emotion. For this journal assignment, find at least three quotations, sayings, song lyrics, poems, or short stories that describe love as you do. Note the pieces you chose and describe why you chose these particular works. What do they say about love that you also believe?

RESOURCES

Bach, R. (1984). The Bridge Across Forever. New York: Dell.

Bloomfield, H., Vettese, S., and Kory, R. (1989). Lifemates. New York: Signet.

Burns, D. (1985). Intimate Connections. New York: Signet.

Coleman, E. and Edwards, B. (1979). Brief Encounters. Garden City, NY: Anchor.

Colgrove, M., Bloomfield, H., & McWilliams, P. (1976). How To Survive the Loss of a Love. New York: Bantam.

Farrell, W. (1974). The Liberated Man. New York: Random House.

Farrell, W. (1986). Why Men Are the Way They Are. New York: Berkley.

Fisher, B. (1981). Rebuilding. San Luis Obispo, CA: Impact.

Forward, S. (1991). Obsessive Love. New York: Bantam.

Godek, G. (1991). 1001 Ways to Be Romantic. Boston: Casablanca.

Hendricks, G. and Hendricks, K. (1990). Conscious Loving. New York: Bantam.

Maclean, N. (1976). A River Runs Through It. Chicago: University of Chicago.

Myers, D. (1992). The Pursuit of Happiness. New York: Avon.

Olson, K. (1975). Can You Wait Till Friday? Greenwich, CT: Fawcett.

Powell, J. (198). Why Am I Afraid to Tell You Who I Am? Allen, TX: Tabor.

Powell, J. (1982). Why Am I Afraid to Love? Allen, TX: Tabor.

Tannen, D. (1990). You Just Don't Understand. New York: Ballantine.

LESSON 31

FEAR

A Fear Overcome

Purpose To identify what you learned from overcoming a fear in your life.

Objective By experiencing success in facing something you feared, you gain strength and courage. This courage is "transferable." By reflecting on what led you to face and then overcome a previous fear, you are a step closer to successfully facing other fears you may be experiencing.

Instructions Respond to the questions listed below:

1. What was something you feared at one time in your life but have since overcome?

2. What motivated or led you to overcome your fear?

3. What lessons did you learn from facing your fear?

Concluding Remarks

Success is contagious. Success in dealing with one fear supports and encourages your facing and successfully overcoming other fears in your life. Rather than becoming immobilized by your fears, fostering a 'can do' attitude in facing your fears will allow you to continue growing and developing into the person you most want to be. After you complete this activity, ask yourself the following questions:

a. Why do you think people have some difficulty in sharing their fears?

b. Can you identify other motivators that would lead you to face a fear? What might those motivators be for you?

STRATEGIES FOR DEALING WITH MY FEARS

Purpose   To identify strategies you can use for overcoming your fears.

Objective   Fear can be a great immobilizer. One way to overcome fear's power to imprison you is to be prepared for dealing with fear in advance by identifying ways you can overcome it. By planning strategies today to conquer fears you will face in the future, you can escape from becoming immobilized by this emotion.

Instructions   Fear is a normal human emotion and everyone has some fears. However, it is important to not let fear immobilize you. In order to deal effectively with your fears, brainstorm five strategies that you can use to deal with your fears.

1.

2.

3.

4.

5.

Concluding Remarks   Fear is an emotion that has the power to immobilize you if you allow it to do so. You can remove fear's hold on you by creating strategies for overcoming fear in advance of your actually needing them. After you complete this activity, ask yourself the following questions:

a. Describe how having options for dealing with your fears makes you feel?
b. What do your strategies about dealing with fear suggest to you about yourself?

c. What do you better understand about yourself from how you might choose to deal with your fears?

d. What might help and hinder you from putting the strategies you developed into action?

e. What would be the possible consequences of not utilizing any of your strategies the next time you have a fear to overcome?

JOURNAL ENTRY ON FEAR

Describe a failure you have experienced and what you learned from this incident.

RESOURCES

Csikszentmihalyi, M. (1990). <u>Flow</u>. New York: Harper Collins.

Goulding, M.M. & Goulding, R.L. (1989). <u>Not to Worry</u>. New York: William Morrow and Company, Inc.

Jampolsky, G.G. (1979). <u>Love is Letting Go of Fear</u>. Berkeley, CA: Celestial Arts.

McGinnis, A.L. (1990). <u>The Power of Optimism</u>. San Francisco: Harper & Row Publishers.

Powell, J. (1969). <u>Why Am I Afraid to Tell You Who I Am</u>? Valencia, CA: Tabor Publishing.

Rachman, S.J. (1978). <u>Fear and Courage</u>. New York: W.H. Freeman and Company.

Wolpe, J. & Wolpe D. (1988). <u>Life Without Fear</u>. Oakland, CA: New Harbinger Publications, Inc.

LESSON 32

LONELINESS

THE LETTER

Purpose To make connections with family and friends to let them know how you're doing and (hopefully) solicit some responses from them.

Objectives To write letters to family and friends and identify and describe some of the highlights of college life thus far.

Supplies Paper, envelopes, stamps

Instructions

1. Write letters to family and friends telling them about your life at college. Be sure to mention any highlights you've experienced so far and ask them to write you back.

2. Wait for the replies to come in the mail—it's almost guaranteed that they will.

Concluding Remarks We've all been lonely at many different times in our lives. One way to combat loneliness is by hearing from friends and family. Since phone calls are relatively expensive, mail can be an attractive, affordable way to stay "connected" with other people who are important to you. After you complete this activity, ask yourself the following questions:

a. How did you feel as you wrote your letters? Were some easier to write than others? Why?

b. How did you feel when you received replies? Will you continue to write letters? Why or why not?

CONNECTIONS
HERE, THERE, AND EVERYWHERE

Purpose To make "connections" with ten new people.

Objectives To connect, at least on a surface level, with ten people you do not know and to learn that it's not that hard to introduce yourself to people you do not know.

Instructions 1. Your assignment is to meet ten new people this week. They can come from your residence hall, apartment complex, classes, clubs you belong to, student union, or other campus environments. There are only two requirements for this assignment:

Everyone must be a student at your institution.
You must find out something interesting about each person you meet.

2. Answer the following questions. Compare your answers with other people in your class.

What was the most interesting thing you learned about someone?

How do you usually meet new people?

Did you find people easier to meet in a certain type of environment or place? Why do you think this was so?

How can you keep in contact with these people?

Concluding Remarks

Meeting new people is often uncomfortable, yet going "outside your comfort zone" is usually necessary if you're going to make new friends. This is something that usually gets easier to do with practice. After you have completed this activity, ask yourself the following questions:

a. Was this assignment easy for you? Was it hard? Somewhere in between? Why?
b. Are you now more comfortable introducing yourself to people you do not know? Will you continue to make an effort to introduce yourself to new people? Why or why not?
c. What effect did meeting these people have on you? Did it affect your mood at that time? Did it affect your day? Did it affect what you did? Did it affect your life as a whole?
d. How do you think introducing yourself affected the person you met?

JOURNAL ASSIGNMENT ON LONELINESS

Loneliness is an awful feeling and one you will probably experience from time to time in college. Learning to cope with these feelings is an important part of the maturation process. In this journal entry, pretend you're an advice columnist for the student newspaper. You've received the following letter and need to write a response.

Dear Advice Columnist,

I'm a new student in college and I hate it here. I haven't made any friends. Everybody seems stuck up and hangs out with their own cliques of friends. Nobody cares about me or wants to be my friend. What should I do? I'm thinking about dropping out and going home because I'm so lonely.

Signed,
No name please

RESOURCES

Bellah, R., et. al. (1987). <u>Habits of the Heart</u>. New York: Harper and Row.

Bloomfield, H., Vettese, S., and Kory, R. (1989). <u>Lifemates</u>. New York: Signet.

Boyer, E. (1988). <u>Campus Life: In Search of Community</u>. Princeton, NJ: Princeton University Press.

Buber, M. (1958). <u>I and Thou</u>. New York: Charles Scribner's Sons.

Burns, D. (1985). <u>Intimate Connections</u>. New York: Signet.

Coleman, E. and Edwards, B. (1979). <u>Brief Encounters</u>. Garden City, NY: Anchor.

Colgrove, M., Bloomfield, H., & McWilliams, P. (1976). <u>How to Survive the Loss of a Love</u>. New York: Bantam.

Fisher, B. (1981). <u>Rebuilding</u>. San Luis Obispo, CA: Impact.

Forward, S. (1991). <u>Obsessive Love</u>. New York: Bantam.

Hendricks, G. and Hendricks, K. (1990). <u>Conscious Loving</u>. New York: Bantam.

John-Roger & McWilliams, P. (1990). <u>Do It!</u> Los Angeles: Prelude.

Myers, D. (1992). <u>The Pursuit of Happiness</u>. New York: Avon.

Olson, K. (1975). <u>Can You Wait Till Friday?</u> Greenwich, CT: Fawcett.

Peck, M. (1987). <u>The Different Drum</u>. New York: Simon and Schuster.

Peck, M. (1992). <u>A World Waiting to Be Born</u>. New York: Bantam.

Powell, J. (1990). <u>Why Am I Afraid to Tell You Who I Am?</u> Allen, TX: Tabor.

Powell, J. (1982). <u>Why Am I Afraid to Love?</u> Allen, TX: Tabor.

Powell, J. (1985). <u>Will the Real Me Please Stand Up?</u> Allen, TX: Tabor. (Communication focus)

Schlossberg, N. (1990). Marginality and mattering: Key issues in building community. In D. Roberts, *Designing campus activities to foster a sense of community*, <u>New Directions for Student Services</u>, #48, 5-15.

Whitmyer, C. (Ed.). (1993). <u>In the Company of Others</u>. New York: Tarcher/Perigee.

Lesson 33

HAPPINESS

I Am Happy Phrases

Purpose To identify situations that make you happy.

Objective To complete phrases regarding situations that make you happy and reflect on the types of situations that truly make you happy. By being aware of these situations, you can incorporate them into you day to day life and surround yourself with things that make you happy.

Instructions Complete the following phrases.

a. I am happy when _____

b. I am happy with _____

c. I am happy where _____

d. I am happy to _____

e. I am happy about _____

f. I am happy because _____

g. I am happy for _____

h. I am happy being _____

i. I am happy becoming _____

j. I am happy doing _____

k. I am happy feeling _____

l. I am happy thinking _____

m. I am happy watching _____

n. I am happy seeing _____

o. I am happy knowing _____

Concluding Remarks To be happy, you have to know what makes you happy. Once you possess this knowledge, you can take a very active role in making these things part of your daily life. Begin by identifying these items and then take action to make yourself happy today and every day. After you complete this activity, ask yourself the following questions:

a. Are you surprised by how many different things make you happy? Why or why not?
b. How do you feel when you look at all the different things that make you happy?
c. How can you incorporate things that make you happy into your daily life?

CREATING A PERSONAL MANTRA ON HAPPINESS

Purpose To find a way to begin your day with positive thinking.

Objective To create a phrase that you can say to yourself each morning that will allow you to begin your day with positive thinking.

Instructions 1. Create a personal mantra (short phrase) that you can say to yourself each morning that will help you begin your day with positive, happy thoughts. Your mantra may be something a parent said to you growing up, or it could be words to a song that make you happy, or even a phrase that you heard that is significant to you. Write your personal mantra below:

My personal mantra is

2. Post your mantra in a location that you will see each morning such as a mirror or on your closet door.

3. Each morning, say your mantra aloud to yourself several times as you prepare for the day and believe the message that you tell yourself.

Concluding Remarks Many articles have been written on the power of positive thinking. By creating a personal message that you can reinforce for yourself each morning, you can begin your day by "bombarding" yourself with a positive message. Hearing is believing so telling yourself something positive in the morning will translate into a positive experience throughout the day. After you complete this activity, ask yourself the following questions:

a. What made it easy or difficult for you to create a personal mantra on happiness?
b. Do you believe that saying this message aloud to yourself each morning can affect your attitude? Why or why not?
c. What did you learn about yourself from completing this activity?
d. How can you apply this type of positive thinking to other aspects of your life?

JOURNAL ENTRY ON HAPPINESS

Describe the secret of happiness for you and how you try to make this secret part of your life each day.

RESOURCES

Burns, D. (1980). <u>Feeling Good: The New Mood Therapy</u>. New York: Avon Books.

Myers, D. (1992). <u>The Pursuit of Happiness</u>. New York: Avon Books.

Sinetar, M. (1988). <u>Elegant Choices, Healing Choices</u>. New York: Paulist Press.